HERE, RIGHT
MATTERS

HERE, RIGHT MATTERS

AN AMERICAN STORY

ALEXANDER S. VINDMAN

HARPER

An Imprint of HarperCollins*Publishers*

HarperCollins books may be purchased for educational, business, or sales promotional use. For information, please email the Special Markets Department at SPsales@harpercollins.com.

FIRST EDITION

All photos are courtesy of the author unless otherwise indicated.

Library of Congress Cataloging-in-Publication Data has been applied for.

ISBN 978-0-06-307942-7

21 22 23 24 25 LSC 10 9 8 7 6 5 4 3 2 1

To Rachel, Sarah, and Eleanor

CONTENTS

HERE, RIGHT MATTERS

CHAPTER 1

IMPEACHABLE OFFENSE

At 9 a.m., Thursday, July 25, 2019, I was seated with a few other White House officials at the long table in one of the two Situation Rooms in the basement of the West Wing. The bigger room is famous from movies and TV shows, but this room is smaller, more typically businesslike: a long wooden table with ten chairs, maybe a dozen more chairs against wood-paneled walls, and a massive TV screen.

This morning the screen was off. We were all focused intently on the triangular conference call speaker in the middle of the table. President Trump's communications team was placing a call to President Volodymyr Zelensky of Ukraine, and we were here to listen.

I'd been in this room many times, but you don't stop getting a kick out of it. Presidents sit at the head of this table; it was the room where President Obama and his team watched the Osama bin Laden raid being carried out. But as the call was placed, my usual excitement was subdued by a sense that something important had to happen in the next few minutes. While I was hoping that the president's call to President Zelensky would bring to fruition many months of effort to get our national security policy back on track, I was also apprehensive that the conversation would turn into a train wreck.

I was a forty-four-year-old U.S. Army lieutenant colonel assigned to a position equivalent to that of a two-star general, three levels above my rank. Since July 2018, I'd been at the National Security Council, serving as the director for eastern Europe, the Caucasus, and Russia. Recently, deep concerns had been growing throughout the whole U.S. foreign policy community regarding two of the key countries I was responsible for: Russia and Ukraine. We'd long been confused by the president's policy of accommodation and appeasement of Russia, the United States' most pressing major adversary. But now there were new, rapidly emerging worries. This time the issue was the president's inexplicable hostility toward an important U.S. partner critical to our Russia strategy: Ukraine.

Sharing a border with Russia's southwestern boundary, on the flank of the European Union and NATO, Ukraine has been a scene of tension and violence since at least the Middle Ages. Most recently, in 2014, Russia's president Vladimir Putin invaded Ukraine, seizing the Crimean Peninsula, home to millions and representing nearly 5 percent of Ukraine's territory, and attacking its industrial heartland, the Donbass, cleaving even more territory and millions of Ukrainians away from the capital, Kyiv. By 2019, little had changed, Russia's annexation and incorporation of Crimea into the Russian Federation persisted, and Russian military and security forces and their proxy separatists continued to occupy the Donbass. The country's security still precarious, the biggest change was to Ukraine's importance as a bulwark against Russian aggression in eastern Europe. The region could not be more sensitive, volatile, or crucial to U.S. and NATO interests. Ukrainian leaders had recently assured National Security Advisor John Bolton that they were content to play the role of a buffer against Russian aggression; geography left them little choice. But they did request—actually, they insisted—that if Ukrainian blood were to be spilled to defend both the country's independence and the freedom and prosperity of Europe, the least the West could do was support their efforts.

And yet, only weeks earlier, the White House had abruptly put a hold on nearly four hundred million dollars in U.S. security aid that Congress had earmarked for Ukraine. This was money Ukraine badly needed to fend off the continuous threat of Russian aggression on its territory. The abrupt, unexplained White House hold was, therefore, baffling. Not only was it 180 degrees out from the stated policy the entire U.S. government supported, but it was also contrary to U.S. national security interests in the whole region. We'd already gotten used to the president's inattention to any policy, let alone foreign policy, but this sudden White House interest in Ukraine was something new, and was deeply unsettling. We feared that on a whim, the president might send out a barely coherent tweet or make an offhand public remark or an impulsive decision that could throw carefully crafted policy into total disarray—*official* policy of the United States, and thus, in fact, the president's own policy.

For it's not as if President Trump ever made active changes in policy. Indeed, we had never been alerted by the West Wing to any shift in national direction. The official Ukraine policy was, in fact, a matter of broad consensus in the president's professional diplomatic and military administration—so, what exactly, we wondered, was the president doing? How could we advise him to reverse course on this out-of-nowhere hold on crucial funding for Ukraine? If he didn't lift the hold, something could blow up at any time.

In recent weeks, therefore, the whole community of professional foreign policy staff across the U.S. government had been scrambling to sort out what was going on. Everybody, from NSA Bolton to my recently departed boss at the National Security Council, Dr. Fiona Hill, to me—my role was to coordinate all diplomatic, informational, military, and economic policy for the region, across all government departments and agencies—was trying to understand these unsettling developments and to come up with ways of convincing the president of the critical U.S. national security interest in deterring Russian aggression and supporting Ukraine's independence. I proposed and was the driving force behind this interagency security assistance review—which was not, as claimed later by the Oval Office, a review justifying the hold on the funds, but a means of bringing the discussion out of the shadows and into normal foreign policy channels.

By the time I was at the table in the basement conference room on July 25, preparing to listen to the president's call to President Zelensky, my workdays had become consumed by the Oval Office hold on funds. As this was my region, responsibility for organizing a rapid response fell to me. On July 18, I'd managed to convene what we call a Sub-Policy Coordinating Committee, a get-together of senior policymakers for the whole community of interest on Ukraine, from every agency and department, to work up a recommendation for reversing the hold on the funds. By the twenty-first, that meeting had been upgraded to a Policy Coordination Committee, requiring even more administrative and intellectual effort, which convened again on the twenty-third. We even scheduled a higher-level Deputies Committee meeting for the day after the Zelensky call. Chaired by the deputy national security advisor, these meetings bring together all of the president's cabinet deputies and require an enormous amount of advance reading, writing, and coordination.

Due to the confusion over the White House's behavior toward Ukraine, many of us were operating on little sleep, working more than the usual NSC fourteen-hour days. I'd barely seen my wife, Rachel, or my eight-year-old daughter, Eleanor, in weeks.

During that period, I'd discerned a potentially dangerous wrinkle in the Ukraine situation. Actions by the president's personal attorney, Rudolph Giuliani, the former mayor of New York City, suggested a hidden motive for the White House's sudden interest in Ukraine. Operating far outside normal policy circles, Giuliani had been on a mysterious errand that also seemed to involve the U.S. ambassador to the European Union, Gordon Sondland, and the White House chief of staff, Mick Mulvaney. Just a few weeks earlier, I'd participated in a meeting at the White House at which Ambassador Sondland made a suggestion to some visiting top Ukrainian officials: if President Zelensky pursued certain investigations, he might be rewarded with a visit to the White House. These proposed investigations would be of former vice president Joe Biden and his son Hunter: Joe Biden had recently announced his candidacy for the Democratic nomination to challenge Trump for the presidency in the 2020 election. Hunter Biden had previously been on the board of Burisma Holdings, a large Ukrainian natural gas producer.

Ambassador Sondland's proposal was clearly improper. Little could have been more valuable to the new, young, untested leader of Ukraine—the country most vulnerable to Russia—than a one-to-one meeting with the president of the United States, the leader of the free world. A bilateral visit would signal to Russia and the rest of the world a staunch U.S. commitment to having Ukraine's back as well as U.S. support for Zelensky's reform and anticorruption agenda, which was critical to Ukraine's prosperity and to closer integration with the European Union. That's what all of us in the policy community wanted, of course. But making such a supremely valuable piece of U.S. diplomacy dependent on an ally's carrying out investigations into U.S. citizens—not to mention the president's political adversary—was unheard of. Before I'd fully picked up on what was going on, that meeting with the Ukrainians had been abruptly broken up by NSA Bolton, but in a subsequent meeting among U.S. officials, at which Sondland reiterated the idea, I told him point-blank that I thought his proposition was wrong and that NSC would not be party to such an enterprise.

I wanted to believe Sondland was a loose cannon, floating wild ideas of his own, with support from a few misguided colleagues. But he wasn't a freelancing outlier like Giuliani. He was an appointed government official. His maneuverings therefore had me worried.

One other thing made me apprehensive on the morning of President Trump's call to President Zelensky. The call had originally been proposed for July 22, the day after Ukraine's parliamentary elections, and its stated purpose was to congratulate President Zelensky for his party's landslide victory. But the call hadn't been confirmed by White House staff until days later, and it's highly unusual to postpone a pro forma congratulatory call. Then the call was abruptly rescheduled for this morning—also with no explanation.

So on the way over to the White House, I'd made a suggestion to my new boss, Tim Morrison. "You know, we probably want to get the lawyers involved," I said, "to listen in." I meant the NSC legal team. Tim and I were going down the stairs from my third-floor office in the Old Executive Office Building, the massive five-story structure immediately adjacent to the White House, heading for the West Wing basement.

Tim gave me a sardonic look. "Why?" he said, clearly impatient with my suggestion.

"Because this could go all haywire," I replied. We had no idea why the call had suddenly been scheduled—only that Ambassador Sondland had played a role in the scheduling. Having legal on this call might help get any problems under control.

Tim dismissed my suggestion out of hand. Knowing that Fiona Hill had read him in on the July 10 meeting with Sondland, and thinking him wise enough to recognize the risks, I didn't understand his resistance. He'd replaced Fiona only days earlier, and I was still getting used to his management style. Fiona had hired me. Highly regarded in her field, she was a brilliant and thoughtful scholar and analyst with a vast global network. She'd previously served in the Office of the Director of National Intelligence (ODNI) as a national intelligence officer for Russia and Eurasia, and she'd written the book, literally, on Vladimir Putin. Fiona was a great boss—not that we were always in sync: I'd often wanted to be more forward-leaning on policy prescriptions, and with a strong sense of the political minefields, Fiona would pull me back, sometimes to my frustration. Still, we respected and appreciated each other. Fiona expected to leave soon after John Bolton had come in as national security advisor, but then she'd agreed to stay through the fall, then spring, then summer, and maybe even later. Tim Morrison, a Bolton protégé, really wanted the promotion, however, and by June it was clear that Fiona would be leaving.

Caustic and bristling, Tim had little expertise in eastern Europe and Russia. Unlike Fiona, who sought out expert input, he was clearly eager to establish a lot of control and hold matters tightly.

Still, I thought Tim might be willing to push harder and more directly than Fiona had. Maybe we'd work well together. He naturally wanted to get the Ukraine relationship back on track and notch some successes, as did NSA Bolton, and I expected Tim to encourage me to keep organizing the policy consensus for recommending lifting the hold on funds.

And so, despite all my apprehension, as I sat at the conference table and heard the president's call being connected, I had hope, too. This call could well be pleasant, friendly, and productive. The president liked winners, and Zelensky's whole party had scored a landslide win. I knew the president had clear and straightforward talking points—because I'd written them. He was to congratulate Zelensky on his victory, show support for Ukraine's reform and anticorruption agenda, and urge caution regarding the Russians; they would try to manipulate and test Zelensky early on. If President Trump stayed on script, we could begin to get U.S. policy for the region under my purview back where it needed to be. I had some confidence in Zelensky, too. I'd met him in Ukraine; he was funny, charismatic, smart.

The White House operator said, "The parties are now connected."

President Trump began speaking, and I knew right away that everything was going wrong.

That call changed my life.

The first phase of my life was forty-four years long. In that phase, I began life in Soviet Ukraine and lost my mother at the age of three. After my mother's death, our family fled the Soviet Union: my father brought me and my identical twin brother, Eugene; our older brother, Len; and our maternal grandmother to the United States, where we settled in Brooklyn, New York. A top Soviet civil engineer and administrator, my father started over from scratch in America. He raised three boys, did physical labor for a living, learned English, and began to succeed anew in our adopted country.

In that first phase of my life, America lived up to its promise to reward hard work and patriotic dedication. My twin brother and I went to college and then directly into the military and a life of public service to the United States, my older brother joined the Army Reserve, and my stepbrother, Alex, joined the U.S. Marines after high school. Not only the United States but the U.S. Army became my home, and my army career took me to places and put me in positions I never could have imagined: from combat service in Iraq to a diplomatic and Defense Intelligence Agency posting in Moscow; and from the Joint Chiefs of Staff as the political and military expert on Russia to the National Security Council as a director with responsibility for Russia, Ukraine, Moldova, Belarus, and the Caucasus.

By 2019, I was on track for promotion to full colonel. I'd even gained the coveted prize of admission to Senior Service College, colloquially called the U.S. Army War College. I had served, and my service had been rewarded.

The second phase of my life began on July 25, 2019.

I now see that in the lead-up to the call, I'd been suppressing the sneaking thought, triggered by what I'd heard Ambassador Sondland say, that the president of the United States himself might offer President Zelensky U.S. military support and a normalized relationship in exchange for a corruption investigation against two U.S. citizens: Hunter Biden and former vice president Joe Biden. My suppression of that thought had been successful. I never believed I'd hear anything like that.

I certainly didn't know that when I reported what I'd heard—an improper use of presidential power contrary to the foreign policy interests of the United States and undertaken for the president's personal and partisan benefit—I would become responsible for instigating only the third presidential impeachment in our history. I couldn't have known that my decision to testify in the ensuing impeachment hearings would trigger political reprisals, not only against me but also against my twin brother, reprisals that threatened to shake my long-standing faith in the country I'd served for so long. I also couldn't have known that my testimony would inspire a groundswell of public support for my decision, support that has strengthened my faith in America as never before.

As I write this, the second phase of my life is barely a year old. It's been a year of turmoil for the country and for my family and me, in large part because of my decision to report what I heard. I'm no longer at the National Security Council. I'm no longer an officer in the U.S. Army. I'm living in the great unknown, and so, to a great degree, is our country.

But because I've never had any doubt about the fitness of my decision, I remain at peace with the consequences that continue to unfold. My decision was in keeping with everything I was privileged to learn in the first phase of my life from so many sources: my father's courage and focus; our family's emigration from the Soviet Union and struggles in the United States; my career in the U.S. Army and the many impressive senior officers and bosses I've served; the superb foreign policy professionals who have been my colleagues; and the series of demanding and challenging experiences that, first, taught me to grow up and find my purpose in life and, then, placed me at the center of a series of actions that developed my moral compass and sense of responsibility.

It all came together on July 25, 2019, on that call. It all came down to doing my duty.

I couldn't have known that much more difficult decisions lay ahead.

As I listened to the president's voice rising from the conference table speaker, I was rapidly writing in the large green government notebook I used for note taking. And my heart was sinking.

". . . I will say that we do a lot for Ukraine," the president was telling Zelensky, "we spend a lot of effort and a lot of time, much more than the European countries are doing, and they should be helping you more than they are. Germany does almost nothing for you . . ."

The president's tone was detached, unfriendly. He sounded down—his voice lower and deeper than usual, as if he were having a bad morning. He was taking the call in the residence, but that wasn't unusual for him. He was routinely unavailable, and certainly not present in the Oval Office, until late morning or early afternoon. But the early hour couldn't fully account for the president's deliberate, leaden negativity.

Zelensky is a comedian by profession, and he was working hard, making self-deprecating jokes, making fun of his own poll numbers, and saying that he had to win more elections to speak regularly with President Trump. My fluency in Ukrainian allowed me to catch the nuance. As head of state for a vulnerable and dependent country, Zelensky was giving it everything he had, trying to build rapport with the president, flattering a notoriously egotistical character, steering the conversation toward the military aid, and gently trying to elicit the personal White House visit that he and his country so desperately needed.

President Trump just wasn't responsive. Monotone, standoffish, he remained stubbornly aloof to Zelensky's efforts to make a personal connection. I already knew one thing: my carefully prepared talking points had gone by the boards. The president wasn't using them at all. He may never have seen them. As the conversation progressed, my worst fears about the call kept being reconfirmed. Off on a tangent of his own, the president, with every passing moment, was aggravating a potentially explosive foreign policy situation.

And so I did what we in the foreign policy community so often found ourselves doing during the Trump presidency. I began to accept that all our hopes for today's chat had been dashed. The president wasn't moving us toward the all-important and bipartisan goal of lifting the hold on the security funds and enhancing our relations with Ukraine. I had to move on. In the face of the president's erratic behavior, that's what we'd all learned to do. I began mentally walking through new ways to rectify the situation. If the hold on security assistance to Ukraine was not lifted by early August, the Department of Defense would not be able to send the funds required by Congress. I was thinking fast. There was a tentative plan for NSA Bolton to take a personal trip to the region I covered. If Bolton met with Zelensky on that trip, could we get another bite, maybe start shifting things back in the right direction? Maybe the secretary of state, Mike Pompeo, could have a phone conversation with Zelensky and report back to the president that Ukraine was all right? And I could always redouble my efforts to coordinate an interagency position: maybe the unanimity of government certainty that aid to Ukraine is a national security imperative would sway the president, get him to lift his hold on assistance . . .

It may seem surprising that my colleagues and I were busy thinking up ways to pursue a Ukraine policy at variance with the direction that the president of the United States himself now seemed to be taking. But *seemed* is the key word. The policy of firm U.S. support for Ukraine had remained officially in place all along, with the unanimous consent of the secretary of state, all the cabinet deputies, and bipartisan congressional leadership, including the president's most loyal followers, Sen. Ron Johnson, Sen. Lindsey Graham, and the chairman of the powerful Senate Armed Services Committee, Sen. Jim Inhofe. It's true there were these odd, outlying data points contradicting the policy: Giuliani, Sondland, Mulvaney, and their mysterious errand; the hold on funds; the president's negative tone on this call with Zelensky. But these baffling indicators were consistent with a pattern in which the president made ill-conceived decisions only to retract them later.

The fact is that because President Trump never provided any policy guidance, nobody in responsible circles, people far senior to me, ever took his remarks seriously as policy direction. They'd wait to see if anything more substantive confirmed what he'd said, continuing, in the meantime, to pursue agreed-upon directions. As my new boss at NSC, Tim Morrison, had also directed that we continue on course and not treat anything the president might say as a change in policy, there was really nothing else to do. Vital American interests around the world were at stake.

From the speaker, I could hear Zelensky trying to work Trump around to the U.S. security money for Ukraine—the all-important issue for us, too.

"I would also like to thank you for your great support in the area of defense," Zelensky said. "We are ready to continue to cooperate for the next steps. Specifically, we are almost ready to buy more Javelins from the United States for defense purposes." He was referring to a U.S.-made infrared-guided antitank weapon, the Javelin, critical to Ukraine's defense against Russian armored vehicles.

The president didn't miss a beat: "I would like you to do us a favor, though," he said.

I paused in my note taking. What was this?

Very abruptly, the president began rolling out for Zelensky an outlandish, discredited conspiracy theory that Rudy Giuliani had recently been promoting publicly. According to this theory, the 2016 hacking of the Democratic National Committee email server was directed not by the government of Russia, as all U.S. intelligence had shown, but by some rich Ukrainian. The president told Zelensky that he'd like him to look into the matter of Ukrainian actors supposedly behind the DNC server hack. To that end, he asked Zelensky to cooperate with the U.S. attorney general, William Barr. The president also blamed actors in Ukraine for Special Counsel Robert Mueller's investigation of his, Trump's, possible abuse of power and suggested that Zelensky could improve his country's relationship with the United States by pursuing and proving these bizarre allegations.

Not surprisingly, Zelensky took up the subject with alacrity, though he was careful to speak in general terms. "We are open for any future cooperation," he assured President Trump. "We are ready to open a new page on cooperation in relations between the United States and Ukraine." Zelensky responded favorably to Trump's criticism of the recent firing of the corrupt Ukrainian prosecutors Yuriy Lutsenko and Viktor Shokin—"a very good prosecutor," Trump called Lutsenko—and he assured the president that he would appoint a credible, reliable general prosecutor and surround himself only with the kind of people of whom Trump would approve. Zelensky would be happy to see Mr. Giuliani in Ukraine at any time. And, of course, he very much hoped to meet face-to-face with the president himself.

Increasingly unsettled, I'd started taking notes again. I still couldn't get a handle on what was going on, but I'd entirely given up hope for anything positive coming out of the discussion.

"The other thing," the president continued, "there's a lot of talk about Biden's son."

My reaction was visceral. My head snapped up. I looked quickly around the table. Were others tracking this?

". . . that Biden stopped the prosecution," the president explained. Burisma, the Ukrainian company on whose board Biden's son Hunter served, had indeed been investigated. But the investigation had been into activities that took place prior to Hunter Biden's joining. There was nothing to support the allegation that Joe Biden had supported firing the prosecutor Shokin—that he had stopped an investigation, as Trump was now saying—in order to protect his son from investigation; in real life, as everyone in the foreign policy community knew, Shokin had been fired for a *lack* of investigative rigor.

Even if there had been anything to this false Biden story, the president's bringing up any such allegation, against any political rival or any American citizen at all, and demanding an investigation on a call with a foreign head of state was crossing the brightest of bright lines.

But now the president went even further: ". . . and a lot of people want to find out about that," he told Zelensky, "so whatever you can do with the attorney general would be great. Biden went around bragging that he stopped the prosecution, so if you can look into it."

I could hardly believe what I was hearing. I knew that Giuliani had been publicly pushing the false Biden story. And I'd been disturbed to hear Sondland suggest to Ukrainian officials that if Ukraine pursued certain investigations, Zelensky would get a White House visit. Still, for all my long-running concerns about President Trump's approach to Russia, Ukraine, and eastern Europe, and for all of my immediate concerns about how this call with Zelensky might go, I had refused to imagine that I would ever hear a president of the United States ask a foreign head of state—a state dependent on vital U.S. security aid that Congress had earmarked for it, thus binding the executive branch to deliver that aid—to, in essence, manufacture compromising material on an American citizen in exchange for U.S. support. The president was brazenly involving not only himself but also Attorney General Barr, as well as his personal attorney Giuliani, in a wholly improper effort to subvert U.S. foreign policy in order to game an election.

My glance around the table confirmed that I wasn't the only one taking in what was happening. Across from me sat Tim Morrison, who less than an hour earlier had rejected my suggestion to get legal to listen in. A lawyer himself, Tim has an expressive face. He, too, was looking up, eyes darting around. Then he took a deep breath as if to say, "Oh, so it's *that* kind of call."

Jennifer Williams, of the State Department, was sitting next to me at the table. I'm not sure how much she picked up at that precise moment, but later she said that she had a concern. There was also a press officer on the call; she wasn't missing any nuance. A European, and an immigrant like me, she'd served in eastern Europe and knew how certain governments there operated. They operated like this.

Now we knew. This was what Giuliani, Sondland, and Mulvaney had been up to. This was the president's purpose in placing a hold on the funds vital to U.S. security interests. He meant to use lifting the hold as an inducement for Zelensky to dig up dirt on Joe Biden. His real purpose in making this call had nothing to do with repairing Ukraine policy. He was extorting Ukraine to damage a political challenger at home and boost his own political fortunes.

Meanwhile, Zelensky, whose comedy background made him good at reading his audience, was trying to claw his way back to a successful stand-up set. He started kvelling about the time he'd stayed in Trump Tower in New York City; about the Ukrainian friends he had in the United States; about all the American oil that Ukraine was planning to buy; and about the prize: how much he'd like to visit the White House.

And he assured President Trump that he would pursue a transparent inquiry into Hunter Biden.

That was enough. At last the president became friendly, very friendly: "Whenever you would like to come to the White House," he said, "feel free to call. Give us a date, and we'll work that out. I look forward to seeing you."

This was one of Zelensky's key goals for the call, so he expressed delight at the offer and reciprocated by offering to host President Trump in Kyiv or meet him in Poland.

As the call wound down, the president again congratulated Zelensky, in his way. "I'm not sure it was so much of an upset," he said referring to the Ukraine elections, "but congratulations."

"Thank you, Mr. President," said Zelensky. "Bye-bye."

The next thing I remember clearly is being back in the Old Executive Office Building, back on the third floor, and right across from my own office, in the office of the chief ethics counsel for NSC.

This was Yevgeny (Eugene) Vindman, my identical twin brother.

A lawyer, Eugene has had a long military career, including serving as an Eighty-Second Airborne platoon leader and as a judge advocate general (JAG). Our rising careers had kept us apart since our college days, but in 2016, Eugene and I started working in the same building at the Pentagon, and now we were both at NSC, on the same floor, in offices across from each other. We'd been through a lot together, and like most identical twins, we share something of a world of our own. Like many brothers, we can be a bit rowdy with each other, competitive in a friendly way, indulging in some good-natured mock insults. But they say that everybody has a quiet inner voice of good judgment. In my life, that quiet inner voice has been a real person: my brother. Our unique relationship was about to matter even more than it ever had before.

The walk that morning from the White House basement up to my brother's office will always remain pretty much a blur. I do remember looking around the conference room when the meeting broke up, knowing that others, including my boss, had heard what

I'd heard. In that moment, I realized something right away. Nobody else was going to say anything about it. I was the person most knowledgeable about and officially responsible for the portfolio. If I didn't report up the chain of command what I knew, no one might ever find out what the president was up to with Ukraine and the 2020 U.S. election. That's why I went straight to Eugene's office.

I knew what I had to do. I'd known from the moment I heard the president say what he said. Regardless of any impact on the president, the domestic and foreign policy consequences, or personal costs, I had no choice but to report what I'd heard. That duty to report is a critical component of U.S. Army values and of the oath I'd taken to support and defend the U.S. Constitution. Despite the president's constitutional role as commander in chief, at the apex of the military chain of command—in fact, *because* of his role—I had an obligation to report misconduct.

Eugene was the top NSC ethics official, with all the important security clearances. He was therefore uniquely positioned to advise me in the proper procedures for doing the right thing in the right way, and I knew that he would support my doing my duty. He would protect, at all costs, my telling the truth. He would never be swayed by any institutional or presidential interest in covering up the truth.

I made sure to close the door behind me. Eugene, seated behind his desk, was looking at me.

"If what I just heard becomes public," I told my brother, "the president will be impeached."

CHAPTER 2

_____

FROM SCRATCH

_____

My first memories: late 1970s, the Ukrainian Soviet Socialist Republic. Memories like still photographs: looking out a window from a crib in the dacha, the house in the country. Raspberry bushes. Squirming under a fence, trying to get to a river.

Soon after, full-scale memories. But they're not such good ones.

Eug and I—he's still called Yevgeny—are identical twins, three or four years old, and we're living in what feels like an orphanage but is really a sanatorium, supposedly exclusive, for Soviet elites. For us, this grim and lonely institution we've been left in is a chamber of horrors, where reprisal for even mild breaches is harsher and more old-fashioned than most Americans today have experienced. To the staff, we must seem like one kid in two mischievous, adventure-seeking bodies. We're already bold, a bit defiant in the face of authority.

My memory is simply that Eug and I have gotten in trouble yet again. I know because I taste the horrible bitterness of soap in my mouth. This was a favored punishment, having your mouth washed out with soap. It's my first full-scale memory, and Eug's is identical. I also remember staring out the window, wishing our dad would come back.

Only later did we come to understand that we were living there because our mother was in hospice care, dying. Overwhelmed, our father had taken supposedly practical advice and housed us in the institution. Our older brother, Len, had stayed with him.

But my father must have hated our being away from him, and he must have hated that place. One of my next memories is a fast drive that feels like a thrilling escape. Our father is at the wheel of a car, Eug and I are in the back, and we're hurtling down a long driveway, fleeing, never to return.

Soon, with our mother gone, all three of us will be with our father in a far bigger escape, with far higher risks, for higher stakes. In 1979, we'll flee the Soviet Union and immigrate to the United States in search of freedom, equality, and happiness. Like so many others before and after us, we'll become immigrant Americans. We'll begin building new lives in the United States, from scratch. Like so many other American immigrant families, we're used to taking big risks to achieve important goals.

I'm often asked why I made the decision to report what I knew was an improper action taken by the president of the United States. His office alone makes him the most powerful individual in the world.

And this particular president is notorious for personal vindictiveness. While he rewards those whom he deems loyal with pardons for their crimes, he attacks those whom he considers disloyal with firing, vilification, lies, and every kind of illegitimate attempt at reprisal. There were bound to be bad consequences for my decision.

But while going up against President Trump might seem like a tough call, for me, the decision to report what I had heard on the call was instinctual, and I've never reconsidered it. That's because I wasn't intimidated and because I didn't see it as going up against President Trump personally. I was carrying out my sworn duty. In a way, the decision was an easy one. Even if I'd been able to foresee all the dramatic events, both for the American public and for myself, that would follow from my reporting the president's behavior up the chain of command, I wouldn't have hesitated to do it.

Another question I've been asked is how I knew so quickly and firmly what I had to do. Where did I get the moral compass and the courage to act decisively? The answer to that question is really what this book is about. I wasn't born with any special degree of courage or some especially firm moral compass. Nobody is. We become the people we are by learning, and I've learned from every challenging situation I've been lucky enough to face, from every great mentor under whom I've been lucky enough to serve. How I learned to be who I've become, how I knew what I had to do about President Trump's wrongdoing, how I knew how to handle the inevitable fallout that divided my life into two phases—that's the story I want to tell.

It begins with my father and with my ancestry. If the real American Dream is overcoming adversity, my people were doing that before we ever came to America.

My father, Semyon Vindman (pronounced "Simon"), was born on June 25, 1932, to a Jewish family in Kyiv, Ukraine. That means he was born into the epic, tragic history of eastern Europe and Russia at the very moment when that history headed toward a climactic explosion. My being here—not just in the United States, but alive at all—is thanks to some very tough decisions and some high-risk moves made by my ancestors in the face of carnage and chaos I can only imagine.

Ukraine's fascinating, centuries-long history of turmoil and triumph, violence and resilience, involves a highly fraught relationship with Russia. A foreign policy truism puts it succinctly: "Russia without Ukraine is a country; Russia with Ukraine is an empire." By the time I was on that call between President Zelensky and President Trump in 2019, I'd become an expert in that still-fraught relationship. I'd studied it.

My dad, however, had lived it. When he was born, the Soviet Union was carrying on the ancient Russian domination of Ukraine by subjecting the country to what was known as the Great Famine, the deliberate mass killing carried out by Soviet authorities in which millions of Ukrainians died. Then, when my dad was a small child, the Soviet dictator Joseph Stalin carried out the Great Purge, killing and imprisoning millions in Ukraine and throughout the Soviet Union and demolishing the world-class intelligentsia of the city of Kyiv. Nazi Germany, meanwhile, had begun encroaching on eastern Europe more or less unopposed by the Western democratic powers. When my father was seven, Germany, in a pact with the Soviet Union, invaded Poland, Ukraine's neighbor to the west, launching the Second World War. Two years later, Germany broke its pact with the Soviet Union and attacked Russia from Poland.

On June 22, 1941, in an action known as Operation Barbarossa, the Wehrmacht entered Ukraine and began moving with incredible speed, thanks to fast German tanks and Stalin's purge of the Red Army. The first objective was not Moscow but Kyiv, where my family lived. My grandfather, an army officer then only in his late twenties, sent word of the fast-moving Nazi invasion and began preparing. As desperation took over Kyiv, my grandfather told his young wife that they had no choice and no time to lose. She must flee the city with their children—my dad and his sister, six years older—and try to get to Moscow.

The young couple would never see each other again. My grandfather would be killed in the desperate battles against the Nazis somewhere near Kyiv. My grandmother, meanwhile, made it into in a crowd of refugees at the Kyiv train station with her children and only those belongings they could carry. German planes were strafing the station. Nevertheless, a train did make it out of Kyiv that day, and they were on board, riding the tense five hundred miles to Moscow.

There, the Soviet command rejected the whole trainload of Ukrainian refugees. They were not allowed to disembark. The train was turned around and the passengers sent back to almost certain death in Kyiv.

Short of the city, however, my grandmother had gotten her family off the train. They fled farther east, managing to get to the Volga River. There they took passage on a steamboat, heading with other refugees to Samarra, and from there to the remote Ural Mountains. In Chebarkul, in the mountains' foothills, many refugees who had left everything behind (loved ones, possessions, money) shared close quarters and tried to survive.

That's how my dad spent his youth and adolescence. While the Second World War raged throughout Russia, Europe, and Asia, he caught and sold crawfish to bring in money. Food was scarce. To earn what she could for food and shelter, my grandmother spent many hours working at one of the factories that had been dismantled and moved from Ukraine to Chebarkul. My dad joined a group of refugee kids who formed a kind of gang to protect themselves against the local kids. One of the older boys even got ahold of a contraband gun. They did some target practice. Then the KGB found out, arrested the older boys, and sent them to the front.

In 2013, when I was serving as an army attaché to the U.S. embassy in Moscow, I visited Chebarkul. The town is quaint, picturesque. Movie buffs would be reminded of the rural scenes in the film *Doctor Zhivago*: the nineteenth-century wooden structures with big glass windows and smaller windows just above them.

As I walked through the town and countryside, I pondered my father's stories about his childhood flight from Kyiv and his wartime life there in the Urals. I thought about my young grandparents' actions under the terrible pressure of historical events. Tough decision making saved my father from near-certain massacre at a young age. I admire my grandfather for that, and for bearing arms against the Nazis when Ukrainians and all Russian people bore the brunt of an almost unimaginable sacrifice in World War II casualties. That sacrifice was borne on both sides of my family: my maternal grandfather, too, was killed fighting for Ukraine—in his case, in the famous Battle of Kharkiv, in 1941, when the lives of ninety thousand Russian soldiers were sacrificed to grind down Germany's advance into the Soviet Union.

And I admire my grandmother, a young woman alone with two children, who defied authority and stopped at nothing to get them to safety, then struggled to make a life in a new and largely hostile place, bereft of everything she had left behind. I ended my visit to that town in the Urals with renewed appreciation for her struggle and for all my ancestors' sacrifices for future generations.

In the late 1970s, my father faced up to his own stark decision to flee, as his mother had in the 1940s. He made that decision under pressure not from a terrifying invasion by another nation, but from the systematic workings of his own nation.

Many people come to America fleeing poverty and stifled opportunity. Admirably, they're seeking a better chance economically, especially for their children. My family has a different story. My dad gave up comfort and career fulfillment in order to escape an arbitrary, tyrannical government with a pervasive culture of corruption, reprisal, and falsehood. He sought a life for his sons that would be better not in economic but in moral terms. And like his own mother when she arrived in the Urals with him and his sister, he had to start over from scratch.

Despite his many demonstrated skills and abilities, as a Jew in the Soviet Union my father faced repeated obstacles to rising in the system. Virulent anti-Semitism was a prejudice not restricted to Russian gentiles—it was an active policy of the white-collar Soviet world. To succeed in that world, my father had to take the best possible advantage of every chance he got. An engineer, he would overcome obstacles set up by prejudice and government corruption by working harder and getting better results. He also understood what drove people: he participated fully in the Soviet system of favor, in which when you do something for someone, they're indebted to you. That's how things got done.

Over time, my dad became a civil engineer in Kyiv, and by the time he decided that our family had to flee the Soviet Union for the United States, he was at a senior level for both the city and country. As he moved up, he was well rewarded. I've mentioned my very earliest memories of our dacha. Those homes on the Dnieper River in the middle of Kyiv were a luxury in the Soviet system, developed in the Khrushchev era to help city dwellers supplement their diets by allowing them plots of land for agriculture, usually only a few hours away from town. My dad, granted land in an exclusive spot, built his dacha on the river, with a view of the city.

He had gotten married in the late 1950s—not to my mother, but to a woman descended from Russian nobility. They had a son and then they divorced. One of the costs of our flight from the Soviet Union was our family's losing touch with the older half-brother I'd not seen since I was so little I could barely remember him. Because of the unforgiving attitude of the Soviet government toward those who left, any continued contact from my father would have been a personal hazard to his eldest son.

My father married my mother, Nona Kalmanovich, in 1965. She died in 1978. Because her father had died in World War II, my mother was raised by a single mother—my tough, beloved grandmother—and after the death of her older brother, she became an only child. My mother's family was cultured, especially in music, and I think my interest in art, opera, and literature must have come from that side; my father has always been supremely hands-on and pragmatic to the exclusion of much else. One of the only other things I know about my mother is that she looked like Sophia Loren. I know almost nothing about her background or ancestry.

That may seem strange, but these big holes in family knowledge are common among Russians. The Soviet system was dedicated to mass eradication, not only of people but also of history. More than 10 percent of the population was killed by famine and other government eradication policies, and nearly thirty million Russians and Soviets died in World War II. And in an effort to erase the entire history of the bourgeoisie, the Soviet government destroyed records on an equally grand scale.

I think my mother supported the risky idea of leaving the USSR. Even before she died, my father had started criticizing the system that had made him so successful and in which he'd risen so high. He'd begun his career with a strong belief in the Communist theories he'd been taught in school. But the higher he rose in that system, and the more inside it he got, the more clearly he saw how it really worked. The whole thing was a complex of quid pro quo backroom deal making. There was no questioning of authority. There was constant corruption, lying, and violence, and the state ruled supreme. When my father was growing up, reprisals for any dissent, sometimes even for an unwelcome suggestion, included early death in prison camps known as gulags. Later, thanks to some degree of reform, reprisals included jail terms and, for prominent figures who couldn't easily be imprisoned, incarceration in grim psychiatric facilities.

As a senior administrator in that system, you eventually faced a stark choice. If you ignored and denied what you knew about the evil and incompetence of the system, never questioned authority, and sucked up to the right people, you could continue to prosper. But if you couldn't ignore and deny what you knew—if your moral compass was too true for that—you faced a number of prospects, none of them good.

My father couldn't look away from the realities of what he was involved in—and he knew he would be raising his sons to be involved in those realities, too. And so we fled.

In the 1970s, Soviet anti-Semitism inspired the United States to make a mass grant of refugee status to all Jews leaving the USSR. My father, widowed for just over a year, arrived in New York City on Christmas Day 1979 with Len, age eleven, me and Eugene, age four, and our maternal grandmother, his mother-in-law, in her late sixties. Our grandmother and our father had never gotten along well. Still, he couldn't leave her behind. Intense, sometimes tough, she was an old-school Russian grandma—or "babushka," as they say in Russia, a nickname drawn from the traditional head scarf worn by older women—but she loved us deeply, and we loved her. Besides, my father knew he would need someone to take care of us while he figured out how to feed, clothe, and house our family of five.

When we arrived in the United States, we had only $759 in cash and a couple of suitcases—and that only because we'd sold some things in an open-air market in Italy. After leaving the Soviet Union, we'd spent a number of weeks in Vienna and several months in Rome, waiting for our asylum to be granted so we could receive visas for entry into the United States. The length of this process further depleted my father's resources. Given the financial situation, nobody thought his plan for our survival as a family could possibly work. How did he expect to feed us? What kind of opportunities could we ever have, given the abruptly impoverished condition he'd placed us in? Representatives of the Jewish community, assisting the nonprofit Hebrew Immigrant Aid Society with resettlement, strongly advised him to put us up for adoption.

But he hadn't forgotten the Soviet institution where he'd once left us. He visited one foster home, and after taking a peek inside, he refused even to consider breaking up our family. He was betting on the American Dream—not fabulous wealth, but a fair chance to overcome adversity. And he had the family history to back that bet. New challenges breed resilience. Resilience enables us to cope with adversity. That's a Jewish and Ukrainian quality, but it's also an American quality. We may face differing adversities, but what we share, as Americans, is the fact that, when challenged, so many of us rise to the occasion.

Nothing has shaped me more decisively than my father's determination and optimism in the face of far more daunting challenges. It's in large part from his example that I learned how to do the right thing, even if it meant standing alone, and how to accept the consequences. It's in large part from him that I've learned to be confident in starting over.

I come from people who had to be braver than I've had to be.

CHAPTER 3

LATE BLOOMER

I grew up in Brooklyn, the most populous borough of New York City, in the 1980s, when certain things about life there remained much as they'd been in earlier decades. We got so used to the rattle and roar of the subway trains in our neighborhood, elevated on a track high above our heads, that we barely registered it. There was a constant bustle on the sidewalks outside the neighborhood's six-story 1920s apartment buildings and two-story homes. Older women pushed shopping carts from store to store, gathering the makings of dinner for multigenerational families. In summer, men in undershirts sat outdoors at folding tables playing chess and dominoes. Somebody would open a fire hydrant, and we kids would splash about in an urban water park.

Some of that world still exists today. And yet, as Brooklyn has scaled way up, changing quickly from a backwater, even a punch line, into the world capital of hip and chic, a lot has been lost. Eug and I had the benefit of growing up on those old Brooklyn streets, living the life that city kids had lived for decades before our arrival.

It's true that we grew up in the midst of what some today fear and loathe as the stereotypical "inner city." It's also true that in the 1980s, crime in New York City really was high compared to today. Still, despite perceptions of the city as crime-infested, Eug and I felt relatively safe. We walked to our first public school; we played with our friends outside. We were also alert to any sign of danger, and this gave us the street smarts I've used throughout my life.

As immigrants, we Vindmans were nothing new to Brooklyn. The borough had been built largely by and for the people of the great American immigrant experience of the late nineteenth and early twentieth centuries and from the Great Migration of African Americans from the Jim Crow South. For this reason, my family found ourselves in well-established working- and middle-class residential neighborhoods that were sometimes divided along pretty rigid racial and ethnic lines, yet with the famous melting pot crossovers, too. We Vindmans were among those classed as "new immigrants," a reference to the successive waves of more recent arrivals from the Caribbean, China, and many other places. The Russian émigré experience of the 1980s, however, was a very particular one, in part because of the tense, shifting relationship between the Soviet Union and the United States over the years. That relationship would come into play for me much later: both professionally, as an attaché in Moscow, and personally, in a conflict with my father over my decision to testify before Congress.

One of the first things I took in as a recent immigrant was

American curse words. Like so many immigrants before us, our family was fortunate enough to be able to get a brief toehold with members of our extended family who had arrived earlier. That first winter, we spent a few weeks in an apartment with some older cousins who thought it would be helpful to get me and Eug boned up on the local lingo, words we repeated enthusiastically. My early education in English would blend the curse words my cousins taught us with what I heard watching the new color television my dad had purchased with the last of the money he brought to the United States.

My dad had found a one-bedroom apartment for himself and me and my brothers. As for our grandmother, already in her late sixties, she received a one-bedroom apartment of her own through a social-welfare system that immigrants called "Program Eight" (also known as "Section 8"). In those days, apartments in Brighton Beach were basic, with fading wallpaper and elementary kitchens. We had three beds crammed into a single bedroom, but we didn't really notice the lack of privacy. We also had pretty minimal furniture, but from the start there was that TV. My dad wanted us to have something to watch while he spent long, hard days and evenings away from us.

He had a plan. As usual with him, it required total commitment. First, he needed immediate income. Because his Soviet achievements (degrees, long experience as a senior-level civil engineer, a well-rewarded life) meant nothing in the United States, he found a job doing one of the most basic forms of physical labor: heavy lifting at a second-hand furniture store. The pay was twenty dollars a day, and the store's owner, a disreputable Russian immigrant who had arrived in the United States only a couple years before us, took a cut of my dad's meager wage in exchange for cashing his paycheck, a classic scam. Many of the challenges new immigrants face are often posed by those who arrived earlier, and the new-comers often have no recourse for combating such abuse. I never understood how someone who had lived so recently through his own hard transition to the United States would want to prey on his fellow immigrants and countrymen.

Still, with the furniture store job, my dad achieved the first step in his plan: immediate income, however paltry. His next step was to pass the civil service exam and improve our lives. That would take more time. Meanwhile, he refused, characteristically, to take a handout from anyone or to apply for welfare. My grandmother, however (thanks again to Section 8, for pension-age immigrants), was eligible for some income, and she took it. For multigenerational immigrant families like ours, social welfare was critical. It provided the home that enabled my grandmother to take care of us while my dad worked. A lot of people look down on public assistance as a handout, but when I think about our story as American immi-grants, I appreciate the fact that the United States and New York City had systems in place for helping people like us get on their feet. My grandmother's entitlement allowed my dad to progress toward his long-term project of self-sufficiency and betterment, both for himself and for his family: the American Dream.

When I say my grandmother watched us, I mean it literally. When Eug and I were five, she kept us under her eye at all times. But nobody's eye was watchful enough to keep the two of us perfectly in check. My brother and I were not only inseparable but also mis-chievous, irrepressible, even troublemaking. We had boundless en-ergy, and no fear.

Our first neighborhood was Brighton Beach, right next to Coney Island, with its famous, long-faded beachfront amusement park and boardwalk. By the mid-1970s, these neighborhoods had fallen on hard times. When the Soviet Union lifted its long-standing ban on exit visas for Jewish Russians and Ukrainians, many went to Israel but also to the United States, specifically New York City. As a relatively affordable place to rent apartments, Brighton Beach drew a number of these émigrés.

While no Brooklyn neighborhood is ever fully monocultural, by the time we arrived in 1979, Brighton Beach had become heavily populated by recent immigrant Russian and Ukrainian Jews. It's not surprising. From the beach, you can watch the waves of the Lower New York Bay, which feeds into the Atlantic Ocean, a view that reminded many refugees of the Black Sea port of Odessa— hence the neighborhood's nickname, "Little Odessa." Throughout the 1980s, the neighborhood would see an explosion of Russian stores and restaurants, many with Cyrillic lettering on their signs. On the street, we heard ever-present Yiddish and Russian.

Eug and I quickly became vagabonds of Brighton Beach. There was a lot to do, and we were endlessly inquisitive. We were also unconcerned by any risk to life and limb, forcing our grandmother to constantly chase us down. Unlike many kids today, whose activities are often structured by adults and who have many forms of indoor entertainment, Eug and I were repeatedly crossing boundaries. Intensely physical, we were always in motion—qualities we would have to learn to channel in later years. And because there were two of us, dressed in identical outfits, we often looked like a blur, which made it even harder to keep either of us in line.

Eug and I found it surprisingly easy to get into the dark, labyrinthine basements of the neighborhood's prewar, midrise apartment buildings to explore and run around. Out on the sidewalks, we'd jump fire hydrants. And of course the beach was always right there. We lived on Sixth Street, which runs directly to the long boardwalk on the bay. In those days, you could still get under the boardwalk—and so, of course, we did. We'd also climb on the rocks and jetties, scale the lifeguard towers and jump onto the sand far below. As we got older, our range widened further. Eug and I both still have fond memories of improvising obstacle courses for traversing multiple city blocks without setting foot on the pavement: jumping from and climbing between garages behind multigeneration town houses, identifying our various courses with names like "Slippery," "Steep," "Jumps," and so on. This cityscape, combined with our own creativity, made our world a vast playground.

And so we learned to handle injuries. In those days, even the official playground sets weren't padded the way they are now. Once, at age six or seven, I fell off a swing while trying to arrest it before it hit a little girl running behind me, bashing my wrist on the cement ground in the process. Because I didn't bellow or cry, my dad did the universal dad thing: he told me to walk it off. It wasn't until about forty-five minutes later that he realized how severely I'd hurt myself. A later X-ray revealed I'd broken my wrist and had to have a cast.

As for Eug, once, on the boardwalk, he was run over by a man racing along on his ten-speed—you can't bike there as freely now—and he still has the scar on his head to prove it. Roughhousing in our usual way, Eug once pushed me into the back of a parked 1950s-vintage Cadillac whose sharp tailfins cut me. These were everyday, even expected occurrences. Given how kids are often raised today, this all may sound rough and dangerous—and it was, to a degree—but there was learning involved. Without knowing it, I was discovering independence and freedom—its joys and satisfactions, its bumps and frustrations. Those days in Brighton Beach also taught me the importance of close family connections. From my earliest memories in a bleak Soviet institution, Eug and I were a team not only in exploring the world but also in challenging authority—especially unearned or abusive authority—and as we grew and roughhoused, our closeness only deepened.

Another family member critically important to my life, then and now, was our brother, Len. He was seven years older and, even as a kid, mature beyond his years. Len had taken care of Eug and me from a young age. During our move from the Soviet Union, while we were in Italy, our dad put him in charge of us while he went out on the errands that would bring about the next steps in our journey. It was Len who, on a beach west of Rome, hawked the stuff we'd brought with us to raise funds for the move.

In Brooklyn, Len continued to be a kind of surrogate father, but he had his own ways of keeping Eug and me in line. He didn't intimidate us; he didn't have to. We looked up to him and wanted to be like him, so the last thing we wanted to do was annoy him—or, at least, annoy him too much. He was the holder of the fun, taking us places: to Action Park and Six Flags, amusement parks in New Jersey; and to Floyd Bennett Field, a former airfield with playing grounds. Out there, he'd put us behind the wheel of the car or let us act out dangerous *Starsky and Hutch* scenes riding on the car's hood. He developed our mental agility, too, pitting me and Eug against each other in trivia contests and other brain challenges.

All that time, I was also taking in—again, subconsciously—the strength of my grandmother's love for us. We must have driven her crazy in those early days in Brooklyn, yet her commitment to us never flagged. Hers was a tough and intense love, a love from the old school, from another time and place. In her sixties then, she'd already lived through the Soviet depredations in Ukraine, with her husband's death at the hands of Nazis, her son's death, having to raise her daughter as a single mom, and then her daughter's death. Now she'd left her home to spend the rest of her life in a faraway place with us and a son-in-law with whom she didn't get along. She could be hard, and overreactive to perceived slights, but not with me and my brothers. Indeed, she placed no limits on her commitment to us. She'd hold Eug and me by the hand, one on each side, as we hustled through the Brooklyn crowds. She'd chase us when we ranged too far afield. An excellent cook, she didn't just make us good meals but went out of her way to bake us treats. And like many grandmothers, she spent some of what little money she had to buy us presents. She was a smoker, and long before smoking indoors became largely socially unacceptable, she made it a point to smoke only outside, and never in front of Eug and me.

In 1987, when I was twelve, my grandmother died of lung cancer. It's hard now to imagine how anything good in my life in the United States, with all its challenges and successes, could have taken place without her toughness and courage. I suspect that many immigrants to the United States, and many people born here, have had similar figures in their lives.

My facility with languages would become one of the key skills in my professional career. On calls with President Zelensky and other Ukrainian and Russian officials, I didn't have to rely on the interpreters; I could catch nuances that others missed. I also have basic Spanish, from high school, and on my first U.S. Army deployment, I picked up Korean—though, after twenty years of disuse, it has atrophied.

Somehow, in those early days in Brooklyn, I learned English—beyond the curse words. We spoke Russian at home with our grandmother and dad, but my brothers and I always spoke English with one another, and I have no memory of not knowing the language. I'm sure the TV played a big role—sci-fi nerds, Eug and I loved *Battlestar Galactica* and *Star Trek*—but I did no active learning before starting school. Eug's experience was the same. We were already speaking English in kindergarten and first grade—we attended a nearby yeshiva—and by the time we were enrolled in public school, in second grade, we were fully bilingual.

As with so many things, in this I had it far easier than my dad, who had to study hard and fast to learn English. But studying hard and fast is something that comes naturally to him. While working his full-time, low-wage, physical job, he picked up enough English in six months to take and pass the civil service exam. That seems like a pretty rare accomplishment.

Having become a certified civil servant, my dad immediately sought work in his old field. Based on his decades of experience as a civil engineer in the Soviet Union, he was hired by the Department of Environmental Protection as a junior engineer—despite his senior experience—for the decades-long, multibillion-dollar megaproject to replace and repair the centuries-old New York City water supply.

That's when he started working the really long hours, picking up all the overtime he could and sometimes working back-to-back shifts, including nights and weekends. There were times when we hardly saw him. My dad would stay with the city water supply project for the rest of his career.

In 1982, when I was seven, I got a mother. I have no memory of my birth mother, and my father and grandmother didn't seem to talk about her much; it was probably too painful. I do have vague early memories of a few women around my father in Brooklyn, but clearly these relationships were nothing serious. Then came the person I always have and always will call my mom.

Theirs was something of an arranged marriage. The woman who would become my mom had learned, through contacts in the Brighton Beach community, about a widower interested in remarrying. A date was arranged, and to say it worked out would be putting it mildly. Not only did my dad and mom have instant compatibility, but she loved us kids right away—and she even brought a stepbrother into our lives, also named Alex and three years older than me and Eug. And surprisingly enough, we all got along easily right away. Well, almost all—characteristically, my grandmother gave my new mom no quarter. Still, my mom and stepbrother's arrival in our lives was yet another way I learned to appreciate family cohesiveness.

Soon it was time to move again. For my dad, the hyper-Russianness of Brighton Beach had become a problem.

Our lives were secure now. We were a two-parent family, and my dad was working a steady job. You might think that in Brighton Beach, where we had what might seem like the advantage of a larger community full of people like us, Jewish Soviet émigrés, the Vindmans, having overcome a lot of adversity, would have settled in and rested content. But that's not us.

Brighton Beach was static, stubbornly Russian, resisting assimilation into the larger American culture—or, at least not assimilating quickly enough for my dad. Our family and national history were to sustain us, not define us. Though proud of his heritage, my father felt strongly that we were to be American first and foremost. Insularity was to have no part in his American Dream.

After two years in Brighton Beach, we moved to another Brooklyn neighborhood, Borough Park. If you're not from Brooklyn, this might not sound like much of a move, but in those days, the neighborhoods were like little countries. A few subway stops could change everything.

With this move, I learned another lesson from my dad: Don't just start over; keep starting over. Having grown up in the Urals as a refugee from the Nazi invasion, he didn't stay in the Urals. After our mother got sick, and people thought he couldn't take care of Eug and me, he changed his mind and never took advice like that again; he trusted himself instead. He rose to a senior-level Soviet administrative post and then threw it all away to bet on the United States. Even getting us out of the Soviet Union, at huge risk and effort, wasn't enough for him. Now he had to get us out of Little Odessa, too.

Don't just start over; keep starting over. As I write this, I'm still trying to learn that lesson.

We lived in Borough Park for ten years, near the boundaries of some pretty ethnically homogeneous neighborhoods. To the north, Latino. To the south, Hassidic/Orthodox Jewish. To the northwest, a new Chinese cluster. To the southwest, older Italian Americans. Because we lived on the boundaries, we were now experiencing the city as a mix of many ethnic groups, all of whom considered themselves American. Yet, in some of the more homogeneous white neighborhoods, residents were unfriendly, even hostile, when people of color walked through. This hostility led to some notable incidents of racial violence in the 1980s and '90s. Racism, as a key American problem, is also an American immigrant problem.

We moved many times within that new neighborhood, but this wasn't necessarily part of my dad's plan. The fact was that Eug and I remained irrepressible. We were getting bigger and even more rambunctious, and we made a lot of noise. The places we rented were often apartments in two-family homes with the landlords living downstairs—one of our landlords, I remember, was an older Italian American couple; I also remember a "Mrs. Weiss"—but Eug and I were just too loud for their comfort. So we'd have to move again; our leases weren't getting renewed.

Fortunately, some of our boundless energy began getting channeled into sports. In schoolyards, with the walls of adjacent buildings towering six stories above, Eug and I would play the Brooklyn classic, stickball, as well as the urban form of touch football, on concrete ground and with no pads. My physicality and competitiveness were rapidly developing. I may not have been the most coordinated kid, but I was energetic and already supremely dedicated to winning. The love of activity that prompted us to jump off lifeguard towers and invent and run urban obstacle courses remains with me today. And it was the physical demands of army life that would first draw me to the infantry.

At a young age I also developed a desire, a need, to stand up for myself. That quality, too, had to be learned, and I learned it the hard way. I learned it at school.

Eug and I had started at P.S. 105, in the second grade. Later, we would walk to John J. Pershing Intermediate School. Later still, we would walk or take the bus to Franklin Delano Roosevelt High School. Mostly, our experiences with other kids were positive. We were not only Russian but also Jewish immigrants, and amid the diversity of the Borough Park borderland, we might have expected to confront some anti-Semitic prejudice. Yet my best friend growing up, aside from my brothers, was a Palestinian boy named Sarhan Sarhan. He and I met in middle school and quickly grew close, and even as a Jewish refugee, I always felt at home in his Palestinian home: they were refugees, too. That's another thing I took in through my pores in immigrant Brooklyn: the complexities of ethnic life and identity.

Early on, however, when we were only seven or eight, Eug and I ran afoul of a classic school bully. This was a bad situation, the kind of thing that wears on children. Back then, there was little if any formal adult intervention, no anti-bullying programs, little discussion of the issue. This kid singled us out; he picked on us steadily. This went on for a few years.

Eug and I had not yet had any fights, except with each other. But by fifth grade, I'd had enough. The bully provoked me, and this time, instead of avoiding him or just taking it, I found myself rushing at him and pummeling him in the middle of Mrs. Reilly's class, with all the other kids watching. The fight made a ruckus. One of the other teachers—a Vietnam vet, in fact—heard it and came in to break it up.

I got off easy. I think it was clear to the school staff that the bully was more of a problem than I was. It was rumored that he'd even kicked our principal, Mrs. Thatcher. In any event, the Vietnam vet more or less gave me a pass, but he patted down the bully for weapons. The kid was expelled, and that was the last time I saw him.

He'd been bullying others, too, and after the fight, both Eug and I were heroes for a time. Through both middle and high school, we might not have been the most popular kids, but we had the ability to float among all the different groups and cliques and get along with every type. We were liked and welcomed by the smart kids and the cool kids, and we were friendly with the rougher kids on the blocks we lived on. This ability to mingle comfortably in different crowds would become invaluable to me in the army, which draws so many different kinds of people from so many different regions, but it was something I first discovered on the streets of the city.

There was another thing I had to learn: how to learn. This turned out to be a tough one.

Throughout my teenage years, intense physical activity and competition held far more appeal for me than book learning. It wasn't that I struggled in class; it was that I had no interest. I didn't care. Eug and I shared this early lack of intellectual focus, a kind of inattentiveness, easily collecting a mix of As and Bs regardless of how hard or easy the subject. This apathy toward academia may have been connected to our physicality, to our closeness as twins, or just to a general aimlessness. Looking back, I can see that we likely had attention deficit hyperactivity disorder (ADHD), which was then only beginning to be diagnosed and taken seriously. We scored high on IQ tests, but there was a notable dissonance between our measured intelligence and our academic performance. Unfortunately, Eug and I fed off each other with regard to our ADHD. As early as second grade, teachers and administrators learned not to put us in the same class. Separately, we might be managed, if only to a degree. Together, it was like what happens in *Ghostbusters*, with matter and antimatter streams crossing and everything exploding at the speed of light.

Though school wasn't our main interest, by the fourth or fifth grade, I was placed ahead into honors classes—the work came easily to me, my lackadaisical attitude and lack of focus notwithstanding—but I didn't put anything into my studies and had no ambition to prepare for the intellectual demands ahead. Eug was in honors, too, and he even skipped a grade due to the intervention of a teacher who saw that he could handle the work. To my chagrin, my twin brother would stay a year ahead of me throughout high school, graduating before I did. Of course, I considered this situation deeply unfair—it wasn't academic competitiveness, just brotherly competitiveness—and I have always told Eug that my later successes all stem from a profound need to right this terrible wrong from our childhood years. He doesn't seem to feel any guilt over it.

In high school we might have been doing okay academically—if the standard is managing to get through AP classes—but in our family, where high academic achievement is considered the norm, our apathy made us something of a black sheep seen in double vision. "Don't turn out like the Vindman boys" became a refrain among our extended family. They meant us twins: lazy, unfocused troublemakers who would go nowhere.

Len was totally different; an ace student, he would go on to Dartmouth College. One of our cousins went to Stanford University.

When it came time for me to enter college, Eug's earlier acceptance to the State University of New York (SUNY) at Binghamton, though it was considered the most selective of the SUNY schools, may not have looked all that exciting next to where I would be going. My free ride to American University, in Washington, DC, looked better on paper. But it turned out to be an honor for which I was woefully unprepared.

When I arrived at American, I was still more focused on action than study, and was already being drawn to the military. Eug shared this attraction. This, too, was Len's influence. Eug and I had always looked up to and copied our older brother, the keeper of the fun. When he joined the U.S. Army Reserve Officer Training Corps (ROTC) at Dartmouth and told us about his training and showed us the drills, we hung on his every word and copied every move. He'd take a run, and we'd run, too, giving everything we had to try to keep up with him.

When Dartmouth ended its ROTC program, Len entered basic training. He eventually decided against becoming a commissioned officer, enlisting instead in the Army Reserve and serving with the Eleventh Special Forces Group, stationed in Newburgh, New York. (Special Forces training looked especially exciting to Eug and me.) Later, he went to airborne school, where he was engaged in air-assault drills, including plane jumps and what appeared to us to be a lot of other cool stuff.

But there was a more serious side to our military bent, too. Len had an ethos of service to the United States. Through his choices and his example, he was instilling in Eug and me the idea that we had an obligation to pay back the country that had taken us in. Len could plainly see how desperately we needed structure and discipline. He didn't want Eug and me to remain those underachieving "Vindman boys." Our getting ahead would involve greater seriousness about studying, of course, but the physical discipline involved in military training wasn't to be dismissed, either.

I had no overt thought of a full-scale professional military career. Still, by high school, both Eug and I expected to do a stint as army officers, and when Eug began his freshman year at Binghamton, he joined the ROTC.

At American, I naturally followed in his and Len's footsteps and did the same. The ROTC program was at nearby Georgetown University, and early in my freshman year, officer training became all consuming. I tried out for and won the opportunity to participate in Ranger Challenge, the varsity sport of ROTC, an extra-intensive series of competitions on top of regular military training. Early every morning, I'd engage in mentally and physically grueling workouts that were carefully designed to push competing cadets far beyond what we thought we could do. We'd practice building rope bridges—I can still fashion a wireman's knot in my sleep—and conduct rucksack marches. We'd go to shooting ranges, break down and reassemble weapons, practice water survival. And I was doing all this before attending my first class of the day.

Or, more realistically, *not* attending my classes. Ranger Challenge had become my priority, and I was eager to make every cut and be on the top team competing with other schools. I was physically exhausted by the training, yet totally absorbed by it—and naturally, my academic work suffered. I'd come to American unprepared to handle the academic rigor, yet ROTC took my mind even further from studying. Like many other eighteen-year-olds, I had poor judgment with regard to achieving realistic goals, and I couldn't see the big picture. I couldn't even see the small picture, and it was right under my nose. The consequences of putting Ranger Challenge ahead of my studies were inevitable: I was dismissed from American after three semesters because of bad grades.

My father was deeply disappointed in me; so was Len. My lack of focus, however, was persistent: in fact, I wouldn't overcome it until my mid-twenties, when serving as an army officer. While I didn't enjoy the stigma my family placed on me for my academic failure, even my dismissal from American didn't bother me all that much. I took six months off and got a taste of real life. I rented an apartment in the Park Slope neighborhood of Brooklyn and earned a paycheck as a computer technician.

And yet I still wanted, more than anything, to be commissioned as an army officer. Knowing that a commission would require a college degree, I applied to join Eug at SUNY Binghamton. I was accepted, and I went back to school to try again.

Given a second chance, I was determined not to fail a second time. I would not embarrass myself and my family. Focusing on academic work at Binghamton remained a challenge, but the desire to become an army officer pushed me to do what I needed to do in order to succeed. I attended ROTC at Cornell University, the Ivy League school in Ithaca, New York. Multiple times a week, I'd made the hour-long drive from Binghamton to Ithaca for military history, military studies, and leadership training. I again competed in Ranger Challenge, this time with great satisfaction; among many dozens of ROTC programs, my team placed seventh one year and third another. My love for the physical and mental challenges of military intensity was starting to merge with a sense of responsibility about my academic achievement and my future. Through it all, I remained focused on my goal: an officer commission.

I still planned to serve just a stint as an army officer, not embark on a lifelong military career. I hadn't yet found my passion. For me, only with the discovery of a passion could I begin to really apply myself to a given field, to learn real discipline—or, more precisely, to learn what real discipline was and begin to embody it. That discovery would set me on a path to higher achievement.

The Vindman boys—late bloomers, no question. Once we get going, though, we don't look back.

CHAPTER 4

RIGHT WHERE I WANT TO BE

It's January 2000. I'm arriving in South Korea, a second lieutenant assigned to the 1st Battalion, 506th Infantry Regiment—a regiment and battalion with an impressive record in World War II and Vietnam. Much will soon change in the U.S. military presence around the world. In 2000, however, this regiment, stationed near the historically tense border with our adversary North Korea, was the most forward-deployed U.S. unit in the world. So I'm right where I want to be.

I have the beginnings of an actual goal now: to become a good platoon leader—that's what second lieutenants do. And I have a plan: to achieve my goal via the most intensive military activity available to me. Not only is the 506th Infantry near the border with a major U.S. opponent, but this is an "unaccompanied" deployment. That means no families allowed: no distractions, nothing but training time. I hope to learn everything I can about both infantry operations and leadership, under the most demanding conditions possible, and with a real enemy nearby.

You don't always get your first choice of deployment. After completing the Infantry Basic Officer Leader Course, at Fort Benning, Georgia, I'd been slated to stay stateside. But sometimes you can swap assignments, and a guy assigned to Korea wanted to stay closer to his wife and family. So I'd snapped up his Korea assignment.

Here I am. Everything I'll ever learn about serving my country, and *from* serving my country, starts now.

My impulse to take a challenging assignment in Korea was the beginning of something good. I could see myself changing, becoming more focused, thoughtful, and realistic than in my early college days. But I didn't yet know what that meant or where it might take me. I'd done nothing outstanding. I hadn't led people in difficult situations. But from the intense experiences to come in Korea—good and bad, successes and failures—I began to learn what I could do, and what I couldn't do yet. As a lieutenant, as the saying goes, you don't know what you don't know.

The intensive seventeen-week training course at Fort Benning had prepared us new officers to lead platoons in combat. I was still expecting to do only a three- or four-year stint with the army and then go back to school; I was even thinking about applying to medical school. But I just kept finding the most exciting experiences in the military: new challenges and new assignments and offers too good to pass up. Partly, as I would soon learn, this was because I liked to break things down to understand how they worked; I would later joke that I'd make a poor doctor because I liked to break things. But my impulses in that direction now involved mental as well as physical energy, even a developing mental agility.

When I arrived in Korea, leadership presented the newest challenge for me. At Fort Benning, I'd seen right away that some of my peers had greater discipline than I did. The West Pointers were already well adapted to military life and the values of leadership; they'd spent their college years steeped in a military environment. Cornell's ROTC program has a strong reputation; by competing in Ranger Challenge, I'd gotten a taste for what active-duty infantrymen do. Still, at the level of new-officer training, West Pointers are the ones with the immersive educational experience. We also had graduates of the Officer Candidate School at Fort Benning. Because most of them come up from the ranks of enlisted men, they have active military experience: they've served under the command of both strong and weak leaders and know the good leadership from the not-so-good.

So when it comes to leadership training, it's easy for ROTC grads like me to be seen as second-class citizens. Also, though I was physically fit, mentally tough, and tackled every task with my usual competitive gusto and bravado, my judgment still wasn't great. During Airborne School at Fort Benning, for example, I seriously injured my ankle. Right after that, I was slated to begin Ranger School, the premier infantry training course, one of the toughest in the entire military. Upon completion, soldiers are awarded the coveted Ranger tab, which every infantry officer wants. It's the expected decoration at the outset of an army career. How could I miss out on that? I said nothing about my injury.

Ranger School begins with Hell Week: ceaseless physical exertion (and little to no sleep), hand-to-hand combat, long marches and runs, and overnight land navigation exercises. My ankle was weak, the pain excruciating. I tried to tough it out, but that wasn't a good idea. Eventually, the reality sunk in: the weakness and pain were too intense to allow me to continue to the next phase.

So when I arrived in Korea, an infantry officer assigned to the top assault unit, I had no Ranger tab. Right away, I drew skeptical looks from other officers. I would have to prove myself. It wouldn't be easy.

I was serving directly under a captain in Korea, the commander of a 120-man company, and leading my own antitank platoon of 34 soldiers. We had a real-world job: in the event of an attack by North Korea, we were to hold a designated bridge.

In order to do that, however, we would have to become an effective platoon, and so we constantly drilled, maneuvered, and performed exercises. Conditions were tough. My first winter in Korea was said to be the coldest there in fifty years, and we slept out in the elements or, if we were lucky, in tents. It was total misery. Then summer came—but that was just as miserable, thanks to the nearly unbearable heat and monsoon rains. A monsoon could put half the camp underwater.

There were other hazards. We conducted foot marches—twenty-five hard miles carrying heavy packs—right along the Demilitarized Zone (DMZ) between South and North Korea. There were minefields on both sides of the road, marked by signs. That's helpful, but you didn't ever step off the road, because there was no margin for error. At a high spot known as "the Birdcage," we looked into the shared footprint of two nations, poised in tense opposition, with potentially dangerous ramifications for the entire world.

I set out to prove myself in the highly specified role of air-assault, antitank platoon leader. In essence, this meant learning how to take out enemy tanks. On the attack, an air-assault unit is transported by helicopter into unfamiliar places. Upon landing, the antitank platoons have to be ready not only to function on complicated terrain, but also, critically, to use an array of heavy machine guns, grenade launchers, and antitank missiles, often mounted on Humvees, to destroy the capabilities of the enemy's heavily armored, powerfully armed vehicles defending the ground. The job calls for moving around in a wide variety of difficult and unpredictable conditions, from the most rugged mountains to the most treacherously pitted and muddy rice fields. Even while orchestrating this action, the platoon leader must know where he and the platoon are at all times. Navigation is everything.

Not everything came naturally or easily to me, but my navigation ability was sharp, based in part on my prior training—and maybe even on what I'd learned on the streets of Brooklyn. In Korea, this ability quickly sharpened. I had an instinct for terrain and for seeing multiple ways in and out of situations: if one path is blocked, find or invent another. Instinct feeds skill development. That's a satisfying ability to discover in yourself.

A good infantry platoon leader also needs to be creative, an independent thinker, and imaginative—qualities that civilians don't necessarily associate with military leadership. But creativity, independence, and imagination would become hallmarks of my career—starting from the moment in Korea when I was asked to play a key role in a major training exercise.

In the mock battle, my antitank platoon was to serve on the

opposition, supporting a light-infantry company force facing an air assault. We were to keep a battalion from landing its helicopters and to destroy them if they did.

As light infantry, you're going up against a much more powerful force. This was a difficult task, and with little experience, I puzzled over how to do more with less. I had the guns on my antitank vehicles, of course, but I needed more power and flexibility than these could afford me. Then I realized that we also had supply vehicles. Though they're unarmored and not adapted to the purpose of fighting, I took a chance on a potentially crazy idea, and we mounted heavy, .50-caliber machine guns on our supply vehicles, thus enhancing not only our firepower but also our ability to gain angles on the helicopters trying to land the assault forces.

The attacking helicopters' tactic was to hug the mountains, which made them hard to hit. These aircraft can pop up, shoot, and hide quickly behind terrain. But by using machine guns in this unorthodox way, and firing from a larger number of vehicles, my platoon was able to shoot a couple of those helicopters down. And instead of drawing criticism for my unorthodox approach, I was transferred to a rifle platoon in the company.

My success in that training exercise started something that I would develop later, at far more refined levels and in much more challenging, real-world situations. The key to victory is rarely brute force. The key is agility, creativity, and seeing the big picture. Meeting unexpected challenges takes imagination, vision, and action, and I was beginning to learn the craft involved in bringing those qualities together.

I extended my Korea deployment to eighteen months, continuing my education in the profession of arms. During the big annual training exercise, I planned another light-infantry action: an ambush of an armored company. Knowing something about how to use terrain, I taught my men timing: how to take quick, decisive action. Facing a force three times the size of ours, we almost turned the tide of the simulated battle. In the end, my company and battalion were overwhelmed by a brigade attack, but we bought time for the higher headquarters. The exercise demonstrated the fierce power that a smaller, lighter force can bring when used creatively.

I was excited. Some of my developing abilities were rooted in my infantryman's instinct for always being forward-deployed, on the ground, advancing. The sense of purpose made me focus—really, for the first time. Exercising your craft successfully just feels good. Because it's rewarding, you push yourself further. Some people get that feeling early, in school, but it was new to me. Even more rewarding: I started drawing positive regard from superior officers.

The external discipline imposed by military life taught me much, but real discipline, I was finding, comes from within. It's bred by a strong desire to succeed in mastering difficult systems, knowing the details, taking advantage of opportunities. I'd always wanted to compete and win. Now I was in the best arena for learning what winning required, in the most demanding, complicated, and dangerous situation imaginable: preparing troops for combat. This was an exciting life. It posed the greatest of challenges.

Because Korea had twelve-month tours of duty, with constant rotation of personnel, it was hard to carry out an exercise with a full platoon. Most of our training, therefore, took place at the individual, team, and squad levels, smaller groups broken out of the platoon. Toward the end of my time as executive officer there, however, we managed to train up to the platoon level, and in that context, I found an opportunity to push the boundaries of what was expected and to take another calculated risk, one that would teach me much about the nature of good leadership.

One day, there was a pause in all squad training due to a training accident. A ricochet in a shoot house (a building used for training with live ammunition) had injured a soldier. Typically, any squad-training stand-down order would rule out platoon-level training, too, but I pushed to continue our live-fire exercises, urging my battalion and brigade commanders not to miss the opportunity to perform a full-platoon maneuver. They agreed and sent word to the division commander, Lt. Gen. Russel L. Honoré, a two-star major general from Louisiana, inviting him to watch the training.

Sometimes known as the "Ragin' Cajun," Honoré would later become famous for stepping in to clean up disastrous early federal efforts in response to the devastation caused by Hurricane Katrina; after the 2021 mob attack on Congress, he would be tasked by Speaker Pelosi with leading a review of the Capitol's security measures. High risk was involved in this training operation: fumbling a platoon maneuver under General Honoré's eye, especially during a cease-squad-training order, would not make anyone look good. But Colonel Odom, my brigade commander, saw the opportunity inherent in the risk. An awesome officer whom I'd gotten to know when we worked out together in mixed martial arts, Colonel Odom was bold physically and quick mentally. He inspired and impressed me, not least for his positive response to my platoon maneuver idea.

One of the great advantages of the U.S. military's approach to leadership—one that not all nations' militaries follow but that is applicable in so many leadership situations—is "mission command." Under this Prussian-derived approach to leadership, U.S. officers are informed of the intent of a mission and are given guidance, but it's then up to the individual officer to draw on training, skill, and instinct to figure out how to fulfill the mission. There are doctrines, of course, but they don't prescribe every move an officer makes. After all, under shifting, complicated conditions on the ground, no doctrine can ever dictate every move. With mission command, doctrine serves only as a basis from which to deviate, to improvise.

General Honoré arrived at the training area. Together, my brigade commander and I explained the platoon maneuver to the Ragin' Cajun and got his buy-in. Then we pulled it off. Risking failure, we ended up impressing him. Our exercise that day affirmed that, even when a platoon steps outside expected patterns, many superior officers—the best of them—will appreciate and reward such independent thinking. If you take the risk of saying what's on your mind, try new ideas, and back up those ideas with performance, your superior officers will listen; they'll even encourage you. If they don't, there's a problem—in them and in the system. That's a lesson in leadership.

I was lucky to join the army when I did. Shortly afterward, the United States would become engaged in what has turned into two decades of warfare. In 2000 and early 2001, however—though I was only miles from the border of one of our country's opponents—all we did was train intensively. Those eighteen months in Korea gave me the time and space to develop and exercise the creativity, independent thinking, and imagination that make for good officers and good leaders.

Creativity and independence are nothing, of course, if you forget how to get to Carnegie Hall: practice, practice, practice.

During my testimony in the first impeachment hearings, some viewers commented on a badge I was wearing, featuring a blue rifle; that's the Combat Infantryman Badge. I earned a similar-looking badge during my Korea deployment, the Expert Infantry Badge. It indicates mastery of a wide range of skills: a fast forced march, expert shooting to knock down thirty-six out of forty targets from three hundred meters out, and other challenges. To earn that badge, you are given only two chances at each skill and no more than two first-round failures. On my first try, I got all but one: it turned out I had a bad arm for grenade throwing.

When throwing a grenade, the goal is to lob it precisely into a bunker from a safe (and, therefore, challenging) distance. If you don't have the knack, there's only one way to get it: practice, practice, practice. Earlier in my life, I had done only what I was good at and ignored the things that were hard for me. But for my second and final attempt at the Expert Infantry Badge, I spent hours lobbing grenades into bunkers. And in my second year in Korea, thanks to those hours of practice, and my mastery of other basic infantry tasks, I earned that badge: true blue, no mistakes.

During this period, there'd been another unexpected development in my life: I began reading constantly. Erwin Rommel, the German general and military theorist, wrote brilliantly about his use of terrain in World War I, and about using smaller, lighter forces to take out bigger, heavier ones. In my spare time, I voraciously absorbed Rommel's and others' ideas, always looking for ways to apply them in exercises.

Realistic training was becoming my credo. I liked to use live fire, wanting to get—and for my men to get—a sense of what actual combat felt like. I was learning the craft by teaching it to them. Still, I would find I had a long way to go to learn how best to handle the soldiers under my command. I wanted not just to lead them but also to bring out their capabilities, to get them ready to succeed under pressure. My judgment in that area was by no means fully formed. I was still learning and making mistakes in Korea, including triggering perhaps the most embarrassing incident during my eighteen-month deployment.

It happened during a reconnaissance exercise, when my driver and I were maneuvering a Humvee over very tough terrain with a gunner up top in the turret. The Humvee is a high-mobility vehicle, but it can't go everywhere—a fact I thought I knew. While driving along a dike, a raised strip of land with a low-lying rice paddy on either side, we got into a muddy area, and the ground became precarious. Intermittently, I got out and started "ground guiding," walking in front of the vehicle with the driver proceeding slowly behind me. The driver that day was the kind of soldier whom officers call a problem child, with a feisty attitude and not easy to control. At one point, I got back in the Humvee—I had the commander's position, top-right shotgun—cautioned him about his speed, and warned him to take care. When he said, "I got this," I believed him. Immediately after reassuring me, he rolled the vehicle off the dike and into the muddy rice field.

This was the kind of learning you never forget, the kind where you experience your mistakes in painful slow motion. As the Humvee began its roll, the turret gunner, fully exposed up top, was about to be crushed under its massive weight. I grabbed for him, got a grip on his pants, and hauled him inside the vehicle.

So there we were, upside down inside a turtled Humvee in a muddy rice field. We climbed out, and I took stock of the situation. Hauling out a vehicle that heavy, buried in mud, is like hauling out an eighteen-wheeler. It took six or eight hours to bring in a wrecker, a very large pickup truck with a big enough hauler, but even that couldn't get the Humvee out.

Next, we brought in an M88 Recovery Vehicle, a fifty-ton monster specifically designed to recover tanks. Then we had to bring in another one. In the ensuing tedious, eight-hour operation, we accomplished the rescue of a single Humvee from a field. That's a major investment of effort. If we'd been in combat, that Humvee would have been lost. And if I hadn't moved fast enough, or been in the right position, we might have lost the gunner. Not surprisingly, I took a reputational hit for my Humvee recovery operation—an incident that became known among my fellow officers as "Operation Cabbage Patch."

It's pretty well known that some of the most valuable lessons come from failure. And you're lucky if your worst failures come when you're not under deadly pressure. I think about Operation Cabbage Patch every so often. One lesson I learned from it was "Trust, but verify": just because a soldier assures you he can do something, it doesn't mean he can. I also learned that any error in an officer's judgment can be painfully significant. I was good at taking risks, an ability that was paying off for me, but there can be bad consequences to bad judgments. I hadn't truly grasped this before. Later, in combat in Iraq, when we were confronted with the challenge of operating in irrigated fields full of dangerously precipitous dikes, some U.S. troops died in rollovers. Thanks to Operation Cabbage Patch, I always made sure to think through what we were doing and set up alternative means of escape.

As I was learning my craft, the bigger world started opening up to me, too—the international world whose tensions and alliances and contests I would one day make my area of expertise. During my time off in Korea, I spent little of it in bars; instead, I looked for every opportunity to travel within the country. On longer leaves, I went to Japan, visiting both Tokyo and Kyoto, and to Hong Kong; in 2001, I would travel alone throughout China. I loved being on the move, learning every minute of the day, and getting a handle on new languages. These trips also excited me in ways I would build on later, as I began to see up close the broad scope of global politics.

By early 2001, at the end of my Korea deployment, I was a solid platoon leader. Solid, not superb. Because I'd never been a solid *anything* before, I knew I was onto something. I knew that I could be more than solid, that I had it in me to do better and better.

For the first time in my life, I'd discovered a passion: military leadership. I wanted more than anything to pursue it as far as it would take me. And from that passion, and from my commitment to pursuing it, came what I began to know of discipline, clarity, and integrity.

Back stateside, I returned to Ranger School. This time, I earned my tab.

In 2003, my life changed dramatically: I met Rachel Cartmill.

I was at Fort Lewis now, just south of Seattle, in Washington State, on brigade staff as a training officer. From the excitement of Korea, I'd been plunged into the most tedious job I would ever have in the military: ensuring that training exercises from the brigade level down were resourced. Maybe it was good for me to deal with what felt like minutiae, robbed of the day-to-day intensity that had always fed me. They say that what doesn't kill you makes you stronger, but I didn't like it.

The highlight of being on brigade staff was sharing an office with the irrepressible Capt. Bill Jacobsen. A year or two older than me, with four kids, Bill was soon to be a comrade in arms in Iraq. Tragically, he would die in the Baghdad Christmas bombing in 2004, and his kids would grow up without his warmth, energy, and positivity.

By 2003, the training I was resourcing from my desk in Seattle was being called MOUT, for Military Operations in Urban Terrain. This new training focus reflected the huge shift that had taken place in the world. In 2000 and early 2001, while in Korea, I couldn't have envisioned the terrorist attacks of September 11, 2001, or what would follow from them. I'd been conscious, of course, of the 1998 embassy bombings in Africa and the attack on the USS *Cole* in 2000. But 9/11 prompted an abrupt shift in U.S. military efforts, with a new focus on terrorism and Islamic extremism. Back in Korea, I'd doubted if I would ever see action. Then, in the spring of 2003, a U.S.-led coalition invaded Iraq, and I knew the tedium of my current assignment would soon come to an end.

MOUT reflected the rapid evolution of the U.S. vision of warfare after 9/11. The new idea was to learn how to operate against armies in cities and how to cope with the insurgents among an occupied population. We carried out exercises in shoot houses and learned some basic Arabic—I still remember how to yell "Stop, or I'll shoot!"—but we also engaged in "hearts and minds" training. This combination is often referred to as counterinsurgency operations, or COIN ops. It required connecting with the local population, gaining trust, reducing the chances of enemy recruitment from among them, and separating combatants from noncombatants. We brought in Arabic interpreters and paid close attention to reports from the scene. It was on me to coordinate this training, at both the MOUT and the hearts-and-minds levels.

I was now facing questions of a kind I'd never asked before; so was the whole army. What exactly is our mission? How do we train for it? In 2003, neither I nor the army arrived at very sophisticated answers.

After graduating from Ranger School, I had been ordered to Fort Lewis. On the way there, I picked up my parents, who would join me for the cross-country trek. They were still in New York and not getting any younger, and I wanted to take a trip with them and see the American West, Fort Lewis, the West Coast. We made a plan to drive across the country, and I drove to New York to collect them. And there, the weekend before we left, I was set up on a blind date.

Rachel was a flight attendant based in New York City, but commuting to and from her home state of Oklahoma. When I picked her up at her airport hotel room, for me, it was pretty much love at first sight. I figured I had to look pretty good to her, too. I was straight out of Ranger School. Of medium build, I had lost twenty pounds, partly by giving away my food to other guys, and thus enhancing my peer evaluations. (That, too, is part of the craft.) I felt lean, fit, in fighting shape.

Evidently, I'm no mind reader, because Rachel says her first thought was "Let's get this guy a meal—he's emaciated!" Maybe I looked so gaunt that I needed not only food but also her care.

I drove us into Manhattan. Rachel had spent nearly three years living in Israel, so the conversation gravitated toward world events and travel. In keeping with that theme, we headed to a Middle Eastern restaurant. She ordered in Arabic. Now I was really impressed.

It was an idyllic fall evening in New York City, and after dinner we walked around Greenwich Village. At first glance, our backgrounds couldn't have been less similar. I learned that Rachel's father's family had been in Oklahoma since the Land Run of 1889 and that members of her mother's family had been displaced to Oklahoma in President Andrew Jackson's Trail of Tears. Rachel had lived in the same state until she was twenty-four, in the same town for all but a few years. I'd had a city kid childhood, Jewish and Russian. Hers was a childhood of Friday night football games, church on Sunday, big family Thanksgivings, and Fourth of July parades.

And yet, on second glance, our backgrounds were quite similar. We had a common experience and a shared value: the importance of family. That first night, we discussed a truism that Rachel and I both hold as a basic tenet: People are more alike than they are different. They generally want the same things: safety, economic security, opportunity, and to be treated with dignity. Over the years, Rachel and I have found that when you appeal to those desires, it is easy to find common ground with almost anyone.

Maybe I was head over heels that evening, or my head was in the clouds, or both, because when I was driving Rachel back to her hotel, she looked around and said, "Weren't we just at this intersection? Are we going in circles?" I'm generally very good at navigation, and yet I'd gotten lost. To distract her, I leaned over and kissed her. Neither of us was upset that the twenty-mile return journey took two and a half hours. I dropped her off knowing I had just met a woman full of midwestern charm mixed with drive, intelligence, wit, and a sense of adventure. In army terms, Rachel was badass.

I'd gotten a glimpse of how tough she was. I hadn't seen anything yet.

We spoke by phone the next day. Then I had to leave with my parents for our cross-country trip. According to Rachel, I didn't call her for a full week. (I don't remember it that way, but she's usually correct on details.) My parents and I drove all the way to San Francisco to visit my aunt, my dad's sister, and then up to Fort Lewis, just south of Seattle. A big map of the United States that my dad has on one wall still has the pins and labels marking our route on that drive.

About a month later, Rachel flew in to see me for a weekend. I was living in a recently redone apartment development next to the Tacoma Museum of Glass, with a beautiful view of Mount Rainier. Rachel came down with an ear infection, our weekend turned into a week, and by our third encounter, half my stuff seemed to have disappeared from the apartment, with her stuff taking its place.

Soon, Rachel was staying for weeks at a time, and my place had become the commuting base for her flight attendant shifts. Meanwhile, I was getting myself and our forces ready for deployment to Iraq. By now, my administrative purgatory had moved me up to battalion staff level.

On battalion staff, I took the role of assistant operations officer and started to learn the organization in which I would eventually command a company. Will Edens, a young lieutenant with a new wife and a sunny disposition, was with us in the office for a time and also bound for Iraq. As a platoon leader, he would be killed while on patrol by an improvised explosive device, or IED.

Both Rachel and I already wanted to get married. And yet, while it seems a bit juvenile to me now, I didn't want to marry her before my deployment. The risks were real: I didn't want to imagine her a widowed newlywed. I wouldn't formally propose until after I came home from Iraq, and even then, things wouldn't go exactly as planned.

But first I went into combat.

CHAPTER 5

THE MORAL COMPASS

He watched from a discreet distance as the U.S. Humvee convoy left the combat outpost. The size of this convoy suggested that it might be carrying an important person. It was clearly a reconnaissance patrol: this meant that it would come back to the outpost before returning to its main base.

And so he prepared his attack.

Selecting a spot by the road just outside the outpost, he staged the explosive device in a bicycle and then set the bike beside the road. It looked as if somebody had just walked away from it.

Then he waited.

When the convoy came into view again—on its way back to the outpost, just as expected—he selected the third vehicle as his target. That was training. Watching the first vehicle pass, he mentally triggered the device, to hone his timing. He did the same thing when the second vehicle passed. When the third vehicle passed, he had the timing down.

He set off the device.

There was no memorable sound when the IED tore through the passenger-side door of our lightly reinforced Humvee, filling the cabin with smoke and obscuring my vision. The two or three seconds that passed seemed to last forever.

Then I got my bearings and assessed the situation.

The first thing I saw in the smoke were immobile bodies. Beside me, U.S. Marine captain Adams was incapacitated. I didn't know it yet, but a chunk of his butt was gone and he'd almost lost his arm at the elbow.

I looked for the gunner. He sat slumped in the turret; I couldn't tell if he was alive. The driver was okay, pulling the vehicle up and stopping dead.

"I knew it!" he said despairingly. He was furious with himself. He'd seen the bicycle sitting alone, for no good reason, by the side of the road, and he knew he should have read its anomalous position as likely concealment for an IED. He'd seen it, but he hadn't trusted his gut.

My first thought was: *We're stopped dead in the kill zone.*

October 23, 2004: We were on a joint reconnaissance patrol—my battalion commander, the intelligence officer, and I, with our marine counterparts—outside of Fallujah, the most violent center of insurgent warfare against the Iraqi Interim Government and the U.S.-led coalition that had invaded in 2003 and ended the regime of Saddam Hussein.

Fallujah, a couple of hours outside Baghdad, is one of Iraq's larger cities. Before the war, it had become wealthy: Saddam's elites had retired there, and his Ba'ath Party built several palaces in the area. Located in the center of the Sunni Triangle, Fallujah played a crucial role as former Ba'athist elites, cast out of power with the advent of the Iraq War, organized a potent resistance from the city and as Al-Qaeda's emir in Iraq found fertile ground there from which to organize and run his insurgency.

By the fall of 2004, when I arrived in Iraq, the city was under the control of the insurgents. The First Battle of Fallujah had ended with the withdrawal of U.S. forces, and the insurgency now operated there with impunity. I would be deployed in what became known as the Second Battle of Fallujah, aka Fallujah II, aka Operation Phantom Fury. Lasting nearly two months, Phantom Fury was part of a renewed coalition effort to reclaim the city for the Iraqi Interim Government. This joint U.S.-Iraqi-British offensive, known in Arabic as Operation Al-Fajr (the Dawn), was met by intense enemy resistance marked by frequent organizational and tactical ingenuity—a major defense using weaponry ranging from small arms to heavy machine guns to rocket-propelled grenades (RPG) to mortars to lots of IEDs and booby traps.

The training we'd done in urban fighting techniques had not been misplaced. Led mainly by the U.S. Marines' First Division, the U.S. effort in Fallujah saw day after day of house-to-house firefights and dozens of casualties on both sides. Even when certain areas seemed at least tenuously secured, IED, rocket, and mortar attacks were constant, and frequently deadly. The ever-present booby traps and insurgent tunnels required that we remain vigilant for weeks after any battle. Fallujah II became the most intense conflict of the Iraq War and marked the heaviest urban combat that U.S. troops had seen since the Battle of Huế in Vietnam in 1968.

So here I was again, right where I wanted to be. The U.S. military had a new mission in the world. As a soldier, you always wonder how effective your training will be. If you're a fighter, you want to know how you will stand up in a real fight. Fallujah and Iraq turned out to be what I'd been training for.

I'd arrived in Iraq limping. Days before I shipped out from Fort Lewis, Eug came to see me off, and as was so often the case, our being together led to some trouble.

I'd just gotten a motorboat license, so we decided to get out on the Puget Sound, launching off Tacoma, where the massive supertankers sail in and out of the port. These tankers draw so much water that they create incredibly high wakes, which proved irresistible to us. We decided to see if we could jump the wakes with our fourteen-foot speedboat.

We took one pass, hitting the throttle hard as we neared the towering wave, and nailed it, sailing over the peak and splashing down onto the water's surface, still upright and behind the trough. That was fun. For the next one, we went full speed at the peak, our feet left the deck, and we clung to the windscreen as the boat landed hard with a massive crash at the very bottom of the next oncoming wave. In the process, I compressed the very ankle I'd injured before and that had forced me out of Ranger School the first time.

Eug and I were in our late twenties then. Theoretically, we were grown up. But when together, we still tended to revert to our irrepressible Brooklyn expeditions—now with grown-up power and equipment. We didn't always think things through, and as a result, I showed up to my combat deployment slightly impaired physically.

I arrived in Iraq in the first few days of October 2004 as a battalion assistant operations officer for First Battalion, Fifth Infantry Regiment, First Brigade, Twenty-Fifth Infantry Division, out of Fort Lewis. Speaking of grown-up power and equipment: this was a Stryker brigade, and a Stryker was a force to be reckoned with.

The Stryker was more than just a remarkable new vehicle. It was a new military platform: component parts operating in concert, designed for maneuvering in all conditions, more capable and with more firepower than light infantry, and more maneuverable and with more personnel than mechanized infantry. Each Stryker has eight wheels, making it speedy—far faster than a tracked vehicle like a tank—and while it's not heavy like a tank, it's big, capable of carrying a full rifle squad of nine men armed with medium-weight to heavy weapons.

Given my successes in Korea at using light infantry against much heavier forces, the lightness of the Stryker concept relative to tanks and other, heavier equipment appealed to me. We were armed with .50-caliber machine guns and MK 19 grenade launchers, which can reach out and touch the enemy at significant range. We had the capability to transport seven Javelin antitank missiles and light and medium machine guns. Separate vehicles carried antitank systems and heavy mortars. All units were networked for communications, command and control, and battlefield awareness. Our brigade was a massive formation—about four thousand people—with three infantry battalions, a reconnaissance battalion, field artillery, and a support battalion.

This was the Stryker platform's first use, and ours was only the second Stryker brigade in combat. The platform was originally developed for speed and maneuverability in deploying rifle squads—not for front-line combat. And in Iraq, we would be using this new technology to address the emergency of counterinsurgency. In that context, there was an unanticipated reliance on the Stryker for a new kind of frontline fighting.

Right away, my battalion was detached from the parent brigade, or selected out. That's how we ended up in Fallujah: we were designated a reserve unit, a sign of our battalion's strength. Deployed in support of a wide array of engagements, reserve provides one of an army's most vital strategic and tactical resources. When forming a reserve element—in this case, the corps reserve—you pick your strongest unit, because it will be applied at decisive points: either when things get really bad, in order to regain control and prevent catastrophe; or in the event of potential success, to exploit the advantage. To fulfill that special role, our battalion was sent at first to Camp Taji, north of Baghdad, and from there we were committed as the key reserve unit in support of all kinds of other units, in varying engagements. Again, I was learning craft, and learning fast. In these shifting, dangerous contexts, any margin for error was rapidly narrowing.

As the assistant operations officer for the battalion and only an infantry captain, I had multiple things to take in and sort out on the fly, both at the granular, on-the-ground level and at a larger, conceptual level. I was also learning the actual terrain. In support of operations in northern and western Baghdad, my unit went on every sort of patrol. This involved a sharp learning curve. Everywhere in these rural areas, canals irrigated the fields. With their attendant elevated dikes, they represented a real danger. Indeed, the previous unit had suffered some deaths from rollovers, with vehicles filling with water. Fortunately, Operation Cabbage Patch had enhanced my judgment regarding the risks of operating in such an environment. I knew from that earlier experience that spending time trying to get a Stryker unit out of a field would put us in enormous peril of attack from insurgents.

So we came up with ideas. Stryker drivers, sitting forward in a separate compartment from the vehicle commander, the gunner, and the infantry squad, are especially vulnerable to being crushed, drowned, or trapped. We therefore deployed compressed-air canisters, so the drivers could breathe if they were submerged underwater. We also learned that when dealing with an insurgency that is well hidden within a civilian population and operating using surprise attacks, most of your casualties will be taken in the ramp-up period of an operation, when you're just getting the lay of the land.

There's a rule for avoiding surprise: Be alert to both *the absence of the normal* and *the presence of the abnormal*. The absence of the normal might be a busy shopping area that suddenly empties out. The presence of the abnormal might be the sudden appearance of clusters of military-age males in a given area. As an operations officer, I began carrying out my duties in tactical operations centers, the rooms where all operations on the ground are coordinated. Joining a patrol from a TOC wasn't always the easiest thing to pull off without encountering danger from the insurgent enemy. When I did make the move, I kept a mantra constantly in my head: *Absence of the normal, presence of the abnormal . . .*

Meanwhile, the coalition was ramping up for the big fight to reclaim Fallujah, and soon our battalion was committed to Phantom Fury. We had a key role to play there. Assigned to the Second

Brigade, First Cavalry Division, known as the Black Jack Brigade, we were to relieve the marine battalion responsible for everything north and east of the city. This meant taking total responsibility for securing what we called "the ratlines," the enemy's means of getting supplies in and out and of escaping.

To get ready for that operation, we performed the usual hand-off between units, known as relief in place/transfer of authority, or RIP/TOA. This is a quick but crucial operation. As the outgoing unit of marines was replaced by our incoming unit, there were logistics to go over, reports on local leadership and insurgents to write up or absorb, operations to be carried out jointly by the two units. There was also joint reconnaissance to be done. This is when the leader from the outgoing unit takes the leader from the incoming unit on a patrol to check out all the various combat outposts and advise on the lay of the land.

The patrol consisted of a convoy of Humvees: my battalion commander, Lt.-Col. Todd McCaffrey, rode in one of the vehicles with his marine counterpart; our intelligence officer, Capt. Ed Harris, rode in a vehicle with his marine counterpart; and I, as assistant battalion operations officer, rode in a vehicle with my marine counterpart, Captain Adams. The captain and I were in the third vehicle of the convoy as we rolled out to inspect the combat outposts in the region that was to be under our battalion's purview. When we arrived at Combat Outpost Delta, I found an old friend from the Captains Career Course I'd taken at Fort Benning: Brent, a marine, was serving as company commander there. We left his outpost in the Humvee convoy, to look over the territory under his control, and then headed back. From there, we planned to return to base.

We had almost reached the outpost when the IED hit.

———————

In those few slow seconds after the blast, I took in the bodies slumped in the smoke and heard the driver beating himself up for seeing the abandoned bicycle and not reacting to it. *The presence of the abnormal.*

I knew how such attacks usually go. The insurgents' goal is to disable the vehicle and kill or injure as many soldiers as possible and then to follow up with direct fire on the sitting ducks. A secondary explosion was to be expected, and we were stopped dead. If we stayed there, and if there was a firefight, we'd be done.

I said to the driver, "Keep driving! Get out of the kill zone!"

He did. A bit farther down the road, I had him pull up. In a slightly better position now, we grabbed our assault rifles and established security around the vehicle, the driver oriented to the front right and me oriented to the rear right, the direction from which the insurgent had triggered the IED.

Only now did I notice the blood on my shirt and trousers. I'd been hit and had taken shrapnel, but I don't remember any pain. I didn't even know exactly where I'd been hit. It would turn out that I was bleeding from my leg and shoulder, but I could function. I got ready for a fight. I was clearheaded, amped on adrenaline.

Maybe most important: I was falling back on my training. The only thing to do was to take care of the situation, then render aid. I also kept assessing my condition. My blood was all over the place; still, I seemed to be in fighting shape. As I awaited direct fire, an unexpected feeling of calm settled over me. You never know for sure how you'll react to an attack until it happens. I knew I was reacting as I should.

We had some luck that day. By both training and observation,

I knew that if a firefight was going to take place, it would happen right away, as an IED explosion is only the first move in an ambush. But the thirty- to sixty-second pause after the explosion, as I remained wired for a fight, told me that it wasn't going to happen.

The next thing you think of is a sniper. And if sniping doesn't start, you move on to the third thing: the enemy is sophisticated enough to wait for first responders to show up, in aid of the wounded, and then attack them.

The other vehicles in our convoy would have heard the explosion and rolled straight out of the kill zone. I have a vague memory of placing a call requesting medical attention and of marines pulling up in an unarmored Humvee barely protected with metal plates and rapidly collecting the casualties, including me, and racing to the nearest aid station. There was no further attack.

We all lived. Captain Adams had taken the brunt. As the marines' "guest," I'd been sitting behind the driver, a safer spot, so despite carrying shrapnel, I wasn't badly wounded. (I have no memory of my pain level. That might have been the adrenaline, but there must have been some painkillers involved, too.) Medics patched me up, and after only a couple of hours in the aid station, I went back to work, leaving the station in a marine uniform and carrying my blood-soaked army uniform in a plastic bag. I also had my helmet, which now bore a huge gouge. If I hadn't been wearing it, that gouge would have been in my head, and I'd be dead.

I'd earlier developed a way of communicating with Rachel. I had access to a direct line to Eug, who was working in the U.S. Army Forces Command (FORSCOM) headquarters at Fort McPherson, in Atlanta, and he could alert her quickly with any information about me. Rachel says that when I spoke with her after the attack, I sounded pretty drugged-up and incoherent. All I remember is trying to keep my description of the events as anodyne as possible, so she wouldn't worry too much. The wife of Maj. Omar Jones, my battalion operations officer, called Rachel, too, to offer her support, as did Lisa McCaffrey, the wife of my battalion commander.

I still have both the helmet and the blood-soaked uniform, in the same bag. To Rachel's ongoing dismay, I keep them in a footlocker in our basement.

I learned a lot that day, some of which was at once technical and tactical. But I also gained new insight into the complexity of the international strategic environment where I would soon learn to operate more fully.

Sometimes the huge, ongoing drama of big alliances and enmities can be read in small objects. The type of IED that wounded me turned out to be the cutting edge of a new insurgent tactic, an explosively formed penetrator, or EFP. It's a canister with a plate inside, concave where it faces the explosive. When an explosion slams the concave side outward, it makes the plate convex and forms it into a plasma slug that can punch right through metal. This was a clever adaptation of an earlier device, one designed especially for attacking lightly armored Humvees. The insurgents' choice of the EFP that day was a good one, as we weren't properly equipped for that fight: the marines' Humvees weren't yet heavily factory armored, and the EFP proved highly effective against that kind of target.

What's interesting is that this technology had been developed and supplied by the Iranians. That told us something. Iran is Shia, yet those mounting the defense in Fallujah were rival Sunnis. Clearly, the Sunnis were picking up techniques and equipment funneled from the Shia in Iran.

I've thought back many times to what we might have done wrong that day. I never saw the bicycle; I was too busy talking with Captain Adams. The gunner, we learned later, had seen the bike, too, but like the driver, he didn't trust his gut. While it was natural for them to beat themselves up for this error, it's significant that nobody in the vehicles in front of us responded to the bike's abnormal presence, either. With this near miss, I learned a long-term lesson about always trusting my gut.

The incident also revealed how we all, military and civilian, can let our guards down under certain circumstances without intending to. Because we weren't on combat patrol that day—we were just getting the lay of the land—the nature of the operation affected our mood; you can lose a bit of vigilance when you don't intend combat. Also, before we were hit, we'd gotten almost all the way back to the combat outpost. For no good reason, there's often an unfortunate tendency to relax when a task is nearing completion.

Another lesson: frustration, even flat-out boredom, can lead directly to big trouble. After the marines' handoff to our battalion, we had responsibility for the second-most-active zone in Iraq. But counterinsurgency warfare is really an endless series of uneventful patrols—repetitive, dull, boring—punctuated by brief moments of combat. We were on constant patrols, both within the city and outside it. While you can take casualties in intense fights, you don't always make contact when on patrol. You know the enemy is out there, yet nothing's happening. As a result, your judgment can suffer. One battalion commander in our region reportedly rode around Iraq flying an Israeli flag from his vehicle and blasting provocative messages from a loudspeaker. He was looking to draw contact, start something—anything. His battalion took a lot of casualties.

Some officers overreact to the awful shock of an IED attack like the one we'd suffered, especially when men under their command are killed. When noncommissioned officers under one of my fellow captains, a company commander, were blown up in a vehicle, the captain's response was to detain several members of the local population and intimidate and threaten them, hoping to determine where the attack had come from and who was responsible. For him, it was personal. He wanted retribution. This may have been a natural reaction to the loss of men, but he was violating the law of war and lost sight of the bigger mission: the hearts-and-minds component. By terrorizing members of the local population, he was creating conditions for terrorist recruitment. That captain received a general officer reprimand.

Restraining perfectly natural emotions is part of military professionalism. I faced this issue on one patrol with a platoon leader, in Mosul, early in my deployment. Things on the patrol seemed more or less normal, so we pulled our vehicles to a stop and got out to take a short break. The seeming normalcy of the situation triggered a mild relaxation of vigilance: our vehicles were parked several hundred meters away in a large circle, perpendicular to the street—an ideal position for taking fire.

Suddenly, dirt was getting kicked up right around us. A sniper was firing—and aiming at me. My combat drills kicked right in. I yelled "Sniper!" and we ran to the nearest vehicle. Getting us all in there was like stuffing a sausage casing, but we did it. Then, assembling a picture of where the fire was coming from, we sorted ourselves out and rolled on, searching nearby houses.

In one, we found some military-age males. The platoon leader, pumped up from the experience of taking sniper fire, began handling these guys roughly. "Let's take them in," he said to me. He was certain that they were the ones behind the attack, or at least knew something about it, and he wanted retribution. The men—adolescent boys, really—had no weapons or ammunition. They looked genuinely bewildered, terrified. I couldn't know, of course, that they were innocent of the sniper attack, but I didn't have any evidence of their guilt. Reading their emotional state, I had nothing to trust but my gut.

I put the brakes on the platoon leader's aggression and made the call: release them, I told him. I'll never know for sure if I was right, but you can't let your judgment succumb to adrenaline, anger, or the other emotions inherent in a counterinsurgency environment, where distinguishing between combatants and noncombatants is habitually difficult.

And anyway, regarding the local population, we'd been tasked with winning hearts and minds. It was a controversial policy, but policy wasn't ours to make. Our mission, a difficult one, was to secure our positions without making new enemies. Discipline and professionalism demand doing everything possible to serve the mission—everything. You can't let your guard down, and you can't make it personal.

In the first few days of November 2004, just days into Operation Phantom Fury, the word came down: things in Mosul were going to hell.

The city of Mosul, in the north, was becoming the tipping point for Sunni insurgent activity. It was suspected that Abu Musab al-Zarqawi, the terrorist trainer, was running his show out of Mosul. The United States and Coalition Forces had been trying to cover the entire northern part of the country running all the way out to the Syrian border with only two battalions in the city, a reconnaissance battalion patrolling both another smaller city and a swath of territory out to the Syrian border, and a lightly manned artillery battalion south of Mosul.

My battalion was abruptly directed to disengage right away, in the middle of fighting in Fallujah, and to rejoin, within twenty-four hours, its parent brigade six hundred kilometers away, in Mosul.

Traditionally, you can't move a full-size light or mechanized battalion that far that fast. But we did, and in doing so, our battalion set the template for what's now known as "the Dragoon Ride." In 2015, after Russia annexed Crimea and continued to threaten Ukraine—I would be on the ground in Russia during that invasion—the press gave some attention to long U.S. columns of Strykers suddenly seen moving rapidly across many parts of eastern Europe on highways and back roads alike. This military exercise, dubbed Operation Dragoon Ride, was intended to demonstrate U.S. strength and speed and reassure our allies on Russia's edges.

But the Dragoon Ride was really invented in 2004—not as an exercise, but as an operation. When our battalion disengaged from Fallujah at a moment's notice, handing off its responsibilities to another formation, we traveled six hundred kilometers across insurgent territory at high speed, with almost no breaks, maintaining communication only by satellite, and rolled straight into a fight in Mosul.

At the time, that ride gained renown for demonstrating that a Stryker brigade is the quickest thing the army has for moving everything all at once, both soldiers and weaponry. In 2020, President Trump announced that these very brigades, though they'd played a key role in establishing security in Europe, would be pulled out of Germany to punish Chancellor Angela Merkel.

———————

As the deployment went on, I spent more time organizing, coordinating, and carrying out military operations and less time with combat patrols. Combat happens most directly and obviously on the ground, but orchestrating it, in real time, is how operations take place. That orchestration occurs at a slight remove.

Always be forward—that was still me. Yet discipline and professionalism were introducing me to more sophisticated ways of being forward. As a staff captain, I was developing my skills as an operations officer, playing a demanding game at a high level.

Combat operations are performed at the tactical operations center. I sometimes regard coordinating battles and other military operations as combining the crafts of musical orchestration with conducting. In the TOC, you lay out the plan for each unit's role, then guide the action in real time. And sometimes, when you're responding to a surprise attack or other emergency, you're improvising the score while playing it.

There's nothing glamorous about a TOC. It's basically just a big room with the low, constant hum of highly professional activity: logistics people in one corner and intelligence people in another, both using mIRC, a Windows-based internet relay chat utility, to pick up text message reports from intelligence units or unmanned aerial vehicles (UAVs), aka drones, on what's going on out in the zone. Meanwhile, operations people perform administrative tasks and assign patrols, and communications people connect the TOC, via radio operations and battlefield awareness software, both to higher-ups and to the various platoons on the ground. There are a lot of flat-screens displaying information from many computers, tracking various patrols and other actions. Sometimes a screen will show a feed directly from the drones, too.

In Fallujah, as I stepped up to aid in conducting operations, I found the TOC to be a place conducive to learning quickly and developing skills. You're at the center of everything that's happening, and anything can happen at any moment. Our TOC would get word from above that, say, we needed to set up and carry out a new operation right away. Or our units on the ground would start taking fire, and we'd have to respond.

When the fight starts or a plan goes into operation, it's everybody out—except for the four or five key people necessary to coordinate immediate action. Always professionally calm, the room then falls quiet, with all activity focused on the operation. It's a demanding and intense atmosphere—as I found when, in the spring of 2005, under the supervision of Maj. Omar Jones, we received intelligence that a "high-value individual," a financier of terrorism named Abu Bakar, was in a house within our purview.

This Abu Bakar was an easy call as a target. Because he served the insurgency as a key source of income for weapons and other purchases, catching him would put a serious dent in the insurgents' ability to operate. Special Forces wasn't in a position to move on him, so the job was being handed off to our battalion for immediate action, and for the first time in my career, I found myself unexpectedly at the helm of an unusually high-level operation.

The TOC was very quiet, as usual during an operation, emptied of all but the few necessary people. I was looking quickly at the whole situation via multiple inputs: where our units were, who was available, who could do what, and where the choke points might be. Major Jones, as the operations officer, and Lieutenant Colonel

McCaffrey, as battalion commander, were hovering, watching as I began giving orders for setting up an outer cordon around the subject's reported location. Moving the necessary units into place took more than a matter of minutes. Normally, Major Jones, as the superior operations officer, might suddenly step in and start giving orders to the units himself. So I didn't at first register that he was leaving this to me.

The people on the receiving end of my orders were captains, like me, and company commanders, senior to me. Fleetingly, I imagined some of them hearing my voice and wondering, "Vindman? Why Vindman?" I was in a new role.

Jones was normally a very hands-on guy. But he knew me, and he'd seen me in action in a TOC before. As he kept hanging back and letting me run things, I began to feel a quiet confidence from him. Unless one of my superiors stepped in, I realized, this was going to be all me.

It was an awesome feeling.

I moved more units and had an inner cordon set up. I leaned into my reliance on the others in the room: they, too, would focus on doing their jobs. The immediate task was to move units into place, then carefully, quietly, tighten the cordon, drawing it tighter and tighter until there was nowhere for the subject to go. Then . . . pounce.

I felt Jones and McCaffrey sit back. I had this. I tightened the cordon, tightened it more . . . We were just about to pounce when one platoon moved early. This alarmed the subject, giving away the game. It turned out that there were tunnels under the building. In a flash, he was gone.

We were highly sophisticated, but so was the enemy, and because we jumped the gun, we lost our target. And yet we got very close to catching him—and I'd been left alone to do the work. That operation introduced me to a whole new level of orchestration, and my superiors' confidence in me boosted my own confidence.

Something was happening. I could feel myself hurtling forward, beyond my rank, to new and higher levels of proficiency and professionalism, toward rooms even more critical than the TOC, rooms where the biggest, most important work got done.

I always say that what I know of courage, I learned from my comrades in combat. In Iraq, I gained a new perspective on courage. My peers were continuing to put their lives on the line every day, out on patrols. They were in far more direct danger than I was in the TOC. Lots of friends didn't make it back home.

On December 21, 2004, in Mosul, I'd worked the night shift. Exhausted, I went to sleep and missed being killed. Twenty-two of my comrades died that day in one tragic attack. One was my friend Bill Jacobsen, who left a wife and four kids back at Fort Lewis. In another incident, William Edens, the platoon leader in Alpha Company, assigned to our battalion, was killed in an IED attack while on patrol. These weren't the only friends and peers killed in combat, and I always think about all of them.

In 2019, when I saw that nobody else was stepping up, and it was time for me to take a stand about President Trump's wrongdoing, I felt a responsibility to those people we'd lost. To do the right thing in the right way, I drew on whatever courage I had, on the discipline and professionalism of my service, and on the sacrifices of American service members in recent wars and throughout our history—consequences to myself be damned.

I'd thought I arrived in Iraq with an already strong moral

compass, but I was wrong. The people I knew in my military career, both those who survived and those who lost their lives, helped me form one. What I had to learn about right and wrong, I learned from my fellow soldiers.

There's a saying: Good officers take care of their soldiers. I've met plenty of good officers. And I've met plenty of officers who put themselves and their own well-being ahead of that of their soldiers. I had something to learn about an officer's responsibility to care for their soldiers. That responsibility didn't always come naturally to me.

In my twenties, I still had little experience with the demands and stresses that real life, life outside of military service, can place on soldiers: the conflicting pulls, the post-combat issues, the family problems. Rachel and I seemed on track to get married, but I had no experience of marriage, no kids. A late bloomer, I'd gained a strong focus, which was moving me along fast. I'd become all about my officer career, but I didn't know much about the normal challenges of adulthood.

I'd already led soldiers, but those early lessons of leadership were somewhat conflicted for me. When you're a leader, you're charged solely with fulfilling the mission, and that end sometimes seems to justify any means: you get your soldiers to do what you need them to do and tolerate nothing less and nothing else.

In my first deployment, in Korea, as a new officer in command, I tended to see soldier behavior in black-and-white terms: absolute right versus absolute wrong. As a new officer, you worry about being seen as soft, by the soldiers and by your superior officers. You can overcompensate for that worry, and that's what I did. When dealing with problem soldiers, I sought punitive justice, with a lot of certainty—no discussion, no excuses—because I was sure of my simple goal: fulfill the mission. I was sure of my own moral compass.

In Iraq, I began to see the toll that service can take on soldiers and the many issues with which they struggle. Later, when I was a company commander, a soldier, PFC Candelo, told me that his father was being deported. His young sister was at home, and she was about to have no parents with her. That soldier eventually died in Sadr City, in the service of the United States. His own father was unable to attend his funeral because he had been deported.

These are people here—that's what I had to learn. Families aren't government issue. In Iraq, I began to internalize a more nuanced approach to justice, a case-by-case way of looking at behavior, one that is more realistic, in the end, than adhering to a rigid set of codes. You're not always going to make the right call; nobody can.

One soldier was caught shoplifting. There was something about him that inspired me to take a calculated risk, and I went lighter on him than I would have done when first in command. He has gone on to have a great army career. But I gave another problem soldier too many chances. Betting wrong, I paid some reputational cost for that misjudgment, both with the other soldiers and with my superiors. Still, I was beginning to work things out.

This marked the real beginning of my forming a moral compass. Back when I saw everything in black and white, I thought morality was simple. That's like having a compass with a needle that can swing only due north or due south—pretty useless for navigation. And navigation is everything, because without sensitivity to your immediate situation, there can be no real morality.

I'd left Korea a solid officer. In Iraq, I started to become something more. At the end of 2005, when my combat deployment was over, I went back to Fort Lewis to ask Rachel to marry me.

CHAPTER 6

NOTHING STARTS WITH US

In the Pacific Northwest, at Cape Flattery, the westernmost point of the contiguous United States, there's a promontory high above the ocean with a stunning sunset view. I'm standing there beside Rachel as we gaze at the red sun sinking into the water. I drop to one knee and take her hand. She turns to me, surprised but not too surprised, clearly moved. I look up. Our eyes meet. "Rachel," I begin . . .

Stop.

Rewind.

That's not what happened.

That's what *should* have happened. After Rachel and I reunited following the deployment and our two years together, it was clear where this relationship was heading. My plan was to pop the question on that promontory, one of our favorite destinations. After we resumed sharing an apartment near Fort Lewis, Rachel became aware that while visiting my parents in New York, I'd stopped off at Manhattan's famous Diamond District. I'm not sure how she knew, but she knew.

I'd bought a ring, but I still intended to propose at the perfect moment, at the westernmost point in the continental United States. I was just waiting for the right excuse to take her up there and didn't want to give anything away. But following up on her suspicions, she asked me a few times what I'd done while in New York. Finally, I just put the fancy box containing the diamond ring in the fridge and waited for her to find it.

She did. And that's the real story of how my marriage proposal was made and accepted. Once engaged, though, we did make the trip out to our romantic spot to mark the moment.

We were married by a justice of the peace less than two months after I returned from Iraq, in a quick civil service wedding in advance of a big family wedding planned for a few months later. This approach isn't unusual for military couples: we needed the documentation so that Rachel could move with me to Germany, my next assignment.

Nowadays, we laugh about how our magical day went. We had to fit the wedding into our busy schedules, so Rachel flew in from the East Coast. But I was so slammed at work that I was actually late picking her up—late for our wedding. "Fine! Let's just get married!" Rachel said when I arrived. She was not pleased, as I doubt any bride would have been. I was stressed. "Fine!" I said. It was one of those "Fine!" "Fine!" spats—like we were already married.

The judge was in a good mood, though. Helping a nice young

couple tie the knot was a happy break for him. He'd been presiding over a murder trial all day.

After almost fifteen years of marriage, Rachel and I have turned out to be the kind of couple who like to laugh both at each other and at ourselves. We tease ourselves and each other and make fun especially of our early foibles as a couple. The fact is, though, Rachel is the perfect match for me, my ideal partner. She is beautiful, tough, independent, smart, and very sexy. One of the traits that first drew me to her was her aggressive, decisive driving. Another was her worldliness: when we first met, she was better traveled than I. I sensed a lot of adventures in our future together.

Rachel's not to be trifled with—if you get on her bad side, watch out. She always pushes me to be better. It was Rachel's grit and courage that sustained me early on, sustained me through the crisis of reporting presidential misconduct and the ensuing impeachment hearings and through the reprisals and tough decisions that started this new phase of my life. I couldn't have done any of it without her.

We began married life in Germany. In 2006, my brigade was ordered to Vilseck, a small town in Bavaria, and was redesignated the Second Cavalry (2CR). I was the commander of Apache Troop, First Squadron, which has as its origins a mounted dragoon unit formed in the War of 1812 and storied service in the Civil War, World Wars I and II, Desert Storm, and other engagements.

This meant I would be leading troops in trainings again. Having served in combat, I amplified my focus on making my trainings as real-life as they could get. I even tried to keep food supplies from getting to the soldiers on maneuvers, because that's the kind of thing that can happen in real life. My NCOs came to see me as a real hard-ass, which prompted one of them to work around me to get food out to the troops. His efforts impressed me, in a way, and taught me another lesson. It turned out there were some real-life limits to how much real-life training I could impose on my troops.

Meanwhile, Rachel and I, as newlyweds, were starting to nest. We had a German Shepherd puppy named Scout, but what we most wanted was a child. Yet our shared intense desire to become parents and raise a family met serious obstacles. In the first six months of our marriage, Rachel had two miscarriages. The first one happened on Mother's Day; she was in Oklahoma visiting her family while I was taking part in a field training exercise. We were disappointed, but at first there was no obvious reason for concern.

The second miscarriage happened a few months later, after we'd moved to Germany; we were in Moscow at the time, attending my older brother Len's wedding. Rachel hadn't even known she was pregnant. She wasn't feeling well, though, so we went to the best expatriate clinic in Moscow, a place that left a lot to be desired: after some tests, they sent us to a hotel, telling us to come back in the morning. Thanks to the petrodollars and state wealth flowing into the hands of oligarchs, the Federal Security Service, and President Putin's henchmen, Moscow was the most expensive city in the world at the time. We were therefore spending the equivalent of eight hundred dollars for a basic room at a Marriott. And the city was chaotic and lawless: drivers going the wrong way up one-way streets, cars double- and triple-parked along the main road leading to the Kremlin, and people blithely smoking beneath No Smoking signs.

The next day, we returned to the clinic. We both recall the doctor's exact words: "Mrs. Vindman," he informed Rachel, "your life is not in danger today."

It was funny at the time, despite the news he then delivered about the miscarriage. It's still funny. Rachel's and my shared ability to find the humor in dark moments has helped sustain our marriage.

We next decided to try in vitro fertilization, and in the late summer of 2008, after a couple of rounds, Rachel was pregnant again. In an ultrasound, we saw and heard what all couples who struggle with infertility long for: a strong little heartbeat. By then, we had moved to the Washington, DC, area, where I was beginning language training in order to become an army foreign area officer (FAO), an expert in the political-military operations of specific regions of the world. Rachel studied Russian while I was learning Ukrainian. We found out that we would be having a baby girl in May. Things looked great.

Then, in the early hours of Sunday, January 11, 2009, Rachel, only twenty-four weeks and two days pregnant, began having pain. I drove her quickly to the National Naval Medical Center in Bethesda, Maryland, where it was determined she was in labor. The doctors saw little chance of stopping the birth. As soon as we were moved to a delivery room, a team of doctors from the Neonatal Intensive Care Unit (NICU) came to speak to us. Because Flippy—that's the nickname we'd given our baby because she was always flipping around during ultrasounds—hadn't reached twenty-five weeks' gestation, we had to make the choice about whether to have her resuscitated after birth.

Scary statistics were given. But even as we spoke, there was the reassuring background noise: Flippy's steady heartbeat. We chose to give her life-sustaining medical intervention.

A few hours later, our daughter—actually named Sarah Abigail Vindman—entered the world. We were parents at last. Rachel's parents arrived a few hours later. Sarah was in an incubator. We couldn't touch her; still, we could stare at her and marvel that she had Rachel's crooked pinky fingers and red hair and my nose. We moved into the Bethesda Fisher House, housing provided for military members and veterans whose family members are receiving medical care. The residence allowed us to be very close to the hospital, where we spent all day, every day. We developed a routine. We'd arrive in the morning, after the nurses' shift change, spend all day with Sarah, and then leave to eat dinner during the next shift change. We'd come back to read her a few books and say good night.

Sarah was stable. The doctors often remarked on how well she was doing for a twenty-five-weeker. Rachel's parents went back to Oklahoma on Saturday; by then, both Len and Eug had joined us.

That Saturday night, however, when we returned to the hospital after the shift change, Sarah's vital signs and labs began fluctuating. Eventually, the doctors suggested that one of us go back to Fisher House to rest. Rachel did, but about a half hour later, I had to call her back. The attending physician sat us down and explained: Sarah had an infection. She wasn't responding to treatment.

She was so tiny, and her little body was fighting so hard, but she was just too sick. Rachel and I held each other and cried, but there was no need for a lengthy discussion. Together, we made the decision to withdraw Sarah from life support.

As dawn broke on the frigid morning of January 18, 2009, we held our baby girl for the first time and said good-bye. Those moments of holding Sarah, and losing her, caused me the deepest and most enveloping pain I've ever experienced.

Losing Sarah gave me a new perspective on the whole process of living life: what really matters. Bad things will happen; there's nothing you can do about that. What matters is how you live through those bad things—how you live, generally. Both the pain and the perspective that losing Sarah gave me are with me for life. The best way I know to honor Sarah and her brief life is to live mine honorably and to the fullest.

I've also experienced great joy. In February 2011, we were blessed when Rachel gave birth to a healthy baby girl, Eleanor Abigail Vindman.

I've been a dad for almost ten years now. I try to carry on what I consider my own dad's legacy to me. Honesty and integrity were critical to him. Eug and I could be mischievous, even intractable at times, but the one thing our dad wouldn't tolerate was deception: lying. I don't think you pass on your values by lecturing your kids about them—at least, that's not the main way. You pass them on by living up to them yourself—as my dad did.

So I've always known that I have to be able to look my daughter in the eye. I have to remain confident that I've done my best to live up to the values I received from my father, which I developed in my own way and now want to pass on to our beloved child. I want Ellie to be proud of her father, as I'm proud of mine.

By September 2012, now a family of three, Rachel, Ellie, and I moved to Russia.

My Russia assignment, the posting of a lifetime, would change my life yet again, bringing me closer to the climactic role I would end up playing at the National Security Council in 2018 and '19. This assignment came about through a series of quick successes and switches. In Germany, I'd been offered the opportunity to advance to assistant operations officer, no longer at the battalion level but for the entire brigade. Maj. Omar Jones—soon to be a lieutenant colonel—who had let me run with the Abu Bakar operation in the TOC in Iraq, pulled me up to brigade staff and introduced me to the brigade operations officer, Maj. James Eisenhower. I quickly earned Major Eisenhower's confidence, and he offered me a job heading into another Iraq deployment.

But I had a new goal: I'd switched the trajectory of my career. I now wanted to be a foreign area officer. Drawn from all the branches of the military, FAOs are trained and educated as experts in foreign nations' and regions' political-military operations. As a young operations officer, I'd taken the coordination and orchestration of military operations at the battalion and brigade levels as far as I could. As an FAO, I could go further, integrating all the strategic, political, cultural, sociological, economic, and geographic considerations for U.S. policy for a particular region. Usually, these careers begin with overseas tours, often attached to embassies. So when Major Eisenhower offered me a posting as the brigade's assistant operations officer, I had to make a choice. I could stay with the infantry, which would delay my transition to a future career as a soldier diplomat, or I could jump into my new career path.

I jumped, and suddenly I was faced with a lot of new challenges. As with my Iraq deployment, my new career dovetailed with big international crises and sharp changes in U.S. policy. In 2008, armed conflict between Russia and Georgia led to a crisis in Ukraine in which the nation's governing coalition fell apart. Russia's relationship to Ukraine makes the latter a linchpin to the region; any crisis in Ukraine also risks a crisis in Europe. In the wake of these events, the U.S. military launched an FAO program for Ukraine. By the time Rachel and I lost Sarah, we were in Washington because I was beginning my training there in that Ukraine program.

FAOs get intense schooling, especially in languages. I already had Russian, so I was studying Ukrainian and the history of the region. My immersion not only in the languages of my ancestors but in all the nuances in the complicated history of Russia, Ukraine, and eastern Europe was thrilling. Again, I'd found a passion that inspired me to excel in my scholarship.

This led to one of the most exciting experiences of my career. In 2009–10, in preparation for my attaché assignment, I was sent on an immersion trip to Ukraine. My official posting was to the U.S. embassy in Kyiv, Ukraine, my father's birthplace. Over twelve months, I traversed the country, north and south, east and west. I also went to just about every corner of the former Soviet Union, and to Turkey and China. But I wasn't traveling alone: my battle and travel buddy, Bob McVey, an army FAO, accompanied me.

This was shortly after the loss of Sarah, and these trips helped take my mind off the pain. Still, Rachel and I were separated for much of this time, and that was challenging. Rachel is very well traveled, but she likes her creature comforts, and these rougher destinations weren't her kind of thing. She was also doing fertility treatments and being extra careful. The separation was especially hard on her. I cut one trip short and came home because we hoped she was pregnant, but it turned out to be an ectopic pregnancy. We kept on going as best we could. And I continued my explorations.

These trips developed my understanding of the region I'd be serving throughout the next decade, turning me into one of the army's most knowledgeable Russia experts—and leading to my presence at that conference table in the White House basement. I was improving my language skills and my ability to navigate unfamiliar cultures. I studied the strategic, bilateral relationships between the United States and each country I visited. You can study history at home, as I did. But I'm still infantry in spirit, and I was discovering, yet again and on a whole new level, that there's nothing quite like being on the ground.

The memories from that period will be with me for the rest of my life: traveling in Turkmenistan, on a Turkmen longneck horse, along the Iranian border; visiting Lake Baikal; trekking on horseback in the most unforgiving taiga in the world; viewing the once-blood-soaked battlefield of Stalingrad. I was journeying right through the heart of my family's history, where my grandfathers had died while defending Ukraine from Nazi invasion, the route along which my young grandmother and her children escaped. I saw the ancient ruins of former civilizations. I touched long-standing cultures, still vital and far older than, and very different from, the culture I knew as a twenty-first-century American.

These are the historical crossroads. Here, mighty conflicts occurred, and immense human creativity thrived. Traveling the Silk Road made me ponder the long centuries of relentless contest that marked the regions traversed by that ancient trade route. It was on that journey that I considered what's known as "the Great Game." For almost the entire nineteenth century, Britain struggled to protect all land routes into its great imperial treasure, India, and vied, in both military and diplomatic terms, with Russia as that country, too, built out an empire in Asia. The strategic bone of contention in the Great Game was Afghanistan, site of war after war.

The doctrine these countries were practicing in the Great Game had, by the nineteenth century, become known as "the balance of power." The principle, whose origins can be traced to the political thinking of ancient Greece, became central to diplomacy in Europe after the Renaissance. As the doctrine goes, all nations' security can be maintained by keeping any one nation from becoming too powerful. Those long, perennial wars of the Great Game in the nineteenth century, and the idea of balancing powers, were ultimately about conflicts between entire national psychologies. The national psychology of Russia was to become one of my big subjects.

This was the main lesson from my trip: standing behind all our current tensions are long histories, deep traditions, and complex psychologies. The Baltic states' becoming NATO members is part of a long history that makes their membership also a vulnerability for NATO. The Silk Road region remains among the most fiercely contested areas in the world. With the rise of China, a new Silk Road is developing to connect Asia to all of Europe, and we've seen a revival of the balance-of-power doctrine.

You can't understand any of these developments, or begin to address them in the interest of the United States and of relative stability in the world, if you don't engage with the past on the deepest level. This takes hard work, intense commitment, and close application.

In that context, I'm inspired by the injunction of James Mattis, the blunt Marine Corps general and former secretary of defense. Sometimes called the "warrior monk," Mattis advises learning what he calls "deep" history. "Read about history," the general has said,

> and you become aware that nothing starts with us. It started long ago. If you read enough biography and history, you learn how people have dealt successfully or unsuccessfully with similar situations or patterns in the past. It doesn't give you a template of answers, but it does help you refine the questions you have to ask yourself.

Such respect for the past, and for deeply refined sophistication in understanding it, has been on the wane lately, at least in some circles. That's not good.

In Russia, I would begin to encounter the superb professionalism of the diplomatic, defense, and foreign policy community whose insights were routinely ignored, even derided, by President Trump. That professionalism gives the United States an invaluable resource for fulfilling its role as a global power and leader. Very high levels of expertise have been developed on behalf of service to our country. We ignore and deride that expertise at our peril.

In 2012, I went to Russia to serve as assistant army attaché to the U.S. embassy in Moscow. By the time Rachel, Ellie, and I arrived there, I'd already mastered a new vocabulary. After my Kyiv posting, I'd earned an MA from Harvard in Russian, eastern European, and Central Asian studies. At the Command and General Staff Officers' Course at Fort Lee, Virginia, I'd been named a "Distinguished Honor Graduate." At the Defense Intelligence Agency's Joint Military Attaché School, I learned how to do my job despite the watchful eyes of the Russian security services. Having absorbed all that intellectual and practical training, here I was: back on the ground.

Rachel had dreaded the prospect of a Moscow posting. Her memories of the city were naturally linked to the civic chaos we'd experienced there during her second miscarriage. But we were both impressed right away by the many positive changes in day-to-day life that had been made in the years since. In Moscow, the capital—which is in no way representative of the entire country—cars were no longer parked on sidewalks, shops and restaurants seemed to be thriving, and there seemed to be more order to daily life. That's part of the reason Putin had become and remained popular: he brought order to the country, taking rampant organized crime out of public view and improving everyday life—better roads, reduced traffic, clean parks, and so on. Our family settled in more comfortably than we might have feared.

At work, I was reporting to Brig. Gen. Peter Zwack, the top attaché, a highly experienced intelligence officer and Russia hand. Zwack made me his right-hand man for interactions with the Russians, a situation ripe for new learning. As a military attaché to an embassy, you observe and report on military activities of the host country and pass them up the line. And because everybody knows why you're there, you're constantly surveilled. This was my first direct contact with an authoritarian society—in Russia's case, one run from the top by its security services, including the Federal Security Service, or FSB, a successor to the KGB. In such a state, authorities can enter your home at any time; you have zero expectation of privacy. If your apartment is bugged—as ours was—you know that your marital life is being exposed. Rachel and I did not like that.

In Russia, there's a lot of what some people in the United States call "law and order." In Russia, this, in effect, means not "rule of law," but "rule *by* law," wherein the powerful employ the security state to maintain order and suppress basic freedoms that we Americans take for granted.

Despite the constant surveillance, I gained a deep understanding of Russia's defense and security apparatus, thanks to regular contact with Russian military and diplomatic leadership. On trips throughout the country to observe military exercises, I photographed military parades and equipment, to get to know Russian matériel. I also grew adept at identifying my minders.

Being a native-speaking Russian gave me an advantage: I fit in more easily than most. This and my ease of communication enabled me to accompany one Russian delegation to Washington, DC. On a different delegation trip, I won over my counterparts by taking them skiing.

I think it was my grandfathers' deaths in World War II, however, that gained me the most access. Family history linked me to a number of senior Russian military people. While I surely seemed very American to the older Russian military generation, we shared a historical bond: my immigrant background gave me an edge that few other Americans in my position had. This edge was reinforced in my mind in 2013, when at a defense attaché reception I had put together for families of Russian World War II veterans, I was surprised with a veterans' award, commemorating the seventieth anniversary of the victory, bestowed by the final chief of the Soviet Army General Staff and the head of the largest Soviet Army veterans' group.

Through all these experiences, I was complementing my formal studies with up-close insight into how Russia thinks: its national strategic and military psychology. Russians use fear and intimidation to make the United States second-guess and doubt itself, and thus miscalculate risks. I believe our policy for Russia should be to hold it accountable for its persistent aggression and threats. Yet I also believe in the necessity for dialogue, both to mitigate the disastrous effect of a potential accident or miscalculation and to clearly define the U.S. interests we will defend at all costs. As hard as it is to imagine, there may be prospects for normalizing relations. States are enduring entities, but their interests are changeable. Emperor Alexander I of Russia recognized and supported the early United States. World War II was fought by Allied forces, with the U.S. supporting Russia well before we entered the war. In the future, we may make common cause with Russia again, as we have with Germany and Japan, our World War II adversaries. A common history forms strong bonds.

That shared history, along with a multitude of strategic considerations, gives us strong reasons to continue to talk. For now, we must be laser-focused on deterring Russian aggression and countering Russian malign influence. In the meantime, dialogue keeps the door open for a potentially more collaborative future.

In 2014, I ran right into the Russian knack for intimidation—indeed, for outright aggression—when Vladimir Putin made his moves on Crimea and Ukraine. For this crisis, my infantry and Defense Intelligence Agency training and my developing understanding of Russian military practices were to be tested on the ground.

The Revolution of Dignity that began in the winter of 2014 saw the breakdown of stable government in Ukraine, the Russian seizure of the Crimean Peninsula, and a Russian effort, thinly veiled as a "separatist uprising," in southeastern Ukraine. We all knew exactly what this was: Putin was making a grab for eastern Ukraine and putting the screws to the pro-Western government emerging in Kyiv. And yet what I was positioned to see on the ground, as informed by my studies, was not as plainly evident to the policy community in Washington. History played a huge role in the uprising and the invasion—the kind of "deep" history that General Mattis talks about.

In the summer and fall of 2013, Ukraine was moving toward joining the European Union, a move that was simply intolerable to Russia and a decision that could not stand. It had been clear for a generation after the collapse of the Soviet Union that Russia felt an overriding need to have control over Crimea, which Kyiv sees as part of Ukraine. Moreover, Ukraine's entering Europe would undermine Putin's legacy, kill the Russian effort at a Eurasian economic union, and make a global drama of Ukraine's moving out of Russia's sphere and becoming integrated with European liberal democracy. As several experts have noted, "Russia without Ukraine is a country; Russia with Ukraine is an empire."

These were some of the indicators of what was coming. There were others: As early as 2005, Putin had announced that he considered the collapse of the Soviet Union a great historic tragedy. If you took that speech seriously, you might have anticipated what he ended up doing in Crimea and Ukraine. If you were looking, you could have guessed that Russia would seize the opportunity to take Crimea and, when the Moscow-propped-up separatist uprising fell apart, attack Ukraine in the east.

That's, in fact, what happened. Everybody was shocked by the degree of violence involved in the invasion, but because Russia saw as critical Ukraine's being in its sphere of influence, it was unlikely to have done anything else.

Something I learned from U.S. wavering and uncertainty on Russia and Ukraine in 2014 has stood me in good stead ever since. The United States has always had a hard time understanding how Russian leadership thinks. In risky situations, our lack of understanding creates discomfort, and there's a natural tendency to fill in, conjure up a sense of knowing—not by studying the feared unknown and getting familiar with it, but by choosing a more comforting option: looking in the mirror. We expect a poorly understood adversary to be like us. (This perceiving another through the filter of personal experience is called mirror imaging.) When things then don't go the way we expect, we get into a muddle of anxiety, which leads to self-deterrence. Unable to game out the risks realistically, we fear taking any action at all. We can imagine a million things going wrong, and instead of figuring things out well enough to take some well-calculated risks, we become paralyzed.

The lesson: *Don't self-deter.*

The events of 2014 quickly became a military and diplomatic education not just for me but for everybody involved. The Cold War was long over. All our assumptions of that period had been overturned. Now, more than twenty years later, Russia was again capturing the attention of U.S. leadership. At a certain point on this steep learning curve, I became one of the more knowledgeable people in the army on what the Russians were doing. That degree of expertise would soon send me homeward—as a Russia and Ukraine expert, first at the Joint Chiefs of Staff and then at NSC. For now, though, I was forward, on the scene, closely tracking Russian doctrines for fighting during the "Russian separatist uprising" and the invasion of Crimea—because if you look in the mirror and expect the Russians to fight like you, you won't be able to see what they're actually doing.

In Ukraine, Russia wasn't fighting like us. It was using hybrid warfare: nonlinear combat blending conventional warfare with cyberwarfare, fake news, insincere diplomacy, intervention in elections, and electronic warfare to jam Ukrainian forces' communications. More specifically, the Russians used air ambushes and relied on a lot of indirect fire in the field, with unmanned aerial vehicles firing across borders at unseen targets. The air ambushes were particularly devastating early in the conflict: using man-portable antiaircraft missiles to knock out Ukraine's planes as they took off or landed, the Russians and their proxies basically neutralized Ukraine's air superiority.

Because my obligations as an attaché were focused on understanding Russia's actions in Ukraine and on the Ukraine-Russia border, I started taking weekly trips there during the crisis. I saw Russian hybrid warfare firsthand, collecting and reporting my observations, some of which were included in presidential briefings. As I analyzed these practices, I found that I was learning not only how Russian hybrid warfare works, and not only what Putin was actually doing regarding Russia and Ukraine, but also that all my academic study, while invaluable, would have remained purely abstract if I hadn't been there, on the ground.

I saw things for myself. I knew how to read what I was seeing.

I would have reason to remember that lesson in 2019—and again in 2020.

CHAPTER 7

"I CAN'T BELIEVE YOU DID THAT"

On Election Day 2016, when Donald Trump won the presidency of the United States, I was flying high and diving deep—higher and deeper than I could have dreamed a career as an army foreign area officer would take me. For a little over a year, I'd been playing a key role in developing U.S. military strategy in my region. My ideas would soon start to have an impact at the highest levels, including at the White House. It was a heady time.

I was now assigned to the Joint Chiefs of Staff (JCS). This is the highest-level staff in the military, made up of the most senior and most talented uniformed leaders of all the branches of the armed services. The chairman of the Joint Chiefs advises the president and the secretary of defense, directly, on all military matters. My new post meant I'd be working out of the Pentagon.

When people say "the Pentagon," they often mean the whole U.S. military hierarchy, but the term originally refers, of course, to the famous five-sided building in Arlington, Virginia, headquarters of the Department of Defense. The biggest office building in the world, with almost eighteen miles of corridors, the Pentagon accommodates about 23,000 military and civilian employees, plus another 3,000 support personnel. I was now mastering a profession, operating at enormous scale, critical to the defense of our country.

An assignment to the Pentagon might therefore seem a dream job. But at first, and for the first time, I wasn't exactly where I wanted to be. The job at Joint staff hadn't been on my wish list. I felt I'd found my sweet spot in Russia. My deployment there had connected me to the shifting historical currents and tides of my own ancestry, and it had given me a key job to do in one of international relations' hottest spots. Everything I'd ever learned—from childhood and family life in Brooklyn through training in Korea before 9/11, from combat command and TOC orchestration in Iraq through intellectual immersion in European history—all that had come together in my service as a foreign area officer operating abroad. Because I'd always had the instinct, even when it wasn't ideally channeled, to be on the ground and as close to conflict as possible, when the invasion of Ukraine came, I was perfectly positioned to become one of the most knowledgeable people in the U.S. Army, both on the invasion's deepest background and on Russia's day-to-day military operations.

That felt like the ultimate accomplishment. Maybe I'd found myself.

So my instinct was to stay frontline and to stay foreign—but not necessarily in eastern Europe. There are other volatile locations around the world where U.S. interests confront the most intense challenges. I could envision myself taking what I'd learned in Russia—history, diplomacy, intelligence, and, of course, operations—and applying and developing them elsewhere. I'd been lucky in my assignments so far, generally getting or wrangling my preferences. But this time—no.

I was still only a major. And yet my specific Russia expertise was highly in demand, and coming not from forward positions like Korea, Iraq, and the Russia-Ukraine border, but from home. I got the order to come back. You don't get a say; you go where they tell you, as expressed in the mantra "the needs of the army." There's a matter of duty involved. In the middle of 2015, I was called to the Pentagon to serve the chairman of the Joint Chiefs as an active-duty foreign area officer.

Despite my early misgivings, it turned out that you never necessarily find your sweet spot, as I thought I had overseas. There's always more to learn and unpredictable ways to develop what you learn. You can't perfectly identify the context in which you'll best thrive. Indeed, you may find yourself in new ways if you go where you're needed.

Don't just start over; keep starting over.

At JCS, I began devising and orchestrating the highest-level U.S. military strategy and putting it into operation on a far more expansive range, and at far greater complexity and intricacy, than anything covered by a TOC in combat. Most important, just as with Maj. Omar Jones back in the TOC in Iraq, my superiors were encouraging me to take a leading role. They could recognize the expertise and skills I'd been developing, and far from being threatened, my superiors, both military and civilian, were encouraging me to speak up—and they listened.

From that, I learned new lessons about the nature of good leadership and strong command—and of poor leadership and weak command. All too soon, those lessons would unexpectedly come in handy.

When my Russia deployment ended in June 2015, Rachel, four-year-old Ellie, and I traveled to Israel. This was at once a family vacation and a trip involving my usual preference for thorough coverage of any region I visited. We spent a week in Jerusalem, then another week driving through Galilee and the northern coast. We visited Tel Aviv, took a trip to Eilat, and then I took a day trip to the fortress-like desert city of Petra, famously featured in *Indiana Jones and the Last Crusade*. The city's ancient buildings, theater, former garden—really, a whole ancient city center—were built right into the towering, rose-colored sandstone cliffs. It's a site whose history goes back thousands of years. I joined a tour of the lower third of that extraordinary archaeological and historical phenomenon. Then I had ninety minutes to explore on my own before getting on a bus and heading back to the resort.

I wanted to get to the top of the city. It's a trek—several miles, and several hundred feet of elevation, and the temperature that day was an arid 120 degrees. Still, I had to try, although the guides assured me it's a full-day excursion.

By making it to the top of Petra and back in ninety minutes, I managed to combine a deep immersion in ancient civilization with the kind of fun, personal challenge I still find irresistible. Later, Rachel, Ellie, and I drove through Negev, and then flew back to Moscow to make the move to return home to America.

In our ten years together, Rachel and I had already moved eleven times. Military households have to move, and we get used to it. Still, there's a logistical and emotional challenge every time—and this time it was a family move, with Ellie and our two dogs.

It was also a new kind of move for us: we'd bought a house, sight unseen, in the Northern Virginia suburbs. Sight unseen—that's often a military family necessity, too. As Rachel began the move-in, I was off to Norfolk, Virginia, for a ten-week course for officers assigned to the Joint staff.

The Pentagon was a totally new experience for this army man. No longer training soldiers, no longer in combat, no longer tactical or operational under observation by Russian security service in a volatile conflict zone along Russia's and Ukraine's border, I was impressed into the strategic environment. Now I had a highly demanding officer job with long hours. As an operations officer, I'd already done a lot of administrative desk work, but this was different. I was joining an intellectually super-powered team, a mix of star military officers and superstar civilians. On that team, I was the military's expert in all things Russian. Our task on the Joint staff was nothing less than to shape military strategy and operations for carrying out the all-important Russia policy of the United States.

Russia policy was then in flux. When I joined the Joint staff, about a year and a half before the election of President Trump, the United States was still figuring out its response to President Putin's aggressive posturing in eastern Europe, which had exploded in 2014 with the annexation of Crimea and the invasion of Ukraine. To develop a cogent strategy for dealing with that escalating danger to our allies in the region, and thus to the United States itself, we needed a new and better understanding of Russian motivations, goals, and psychology. Arriving at that understanding, and putting it into operation, became a major part of my job.

The psychology of President Vladimir Putin and Russia's security elites has a deep historical basis. As it has shown again and again in their long history, Russia can grow strong and expand its empire through coercion, leveraging fear and dishing out intimidation to accrue power, perpetuating a cycle of aggression toward its neighbors. Too often, that accrual of power turns out only to mask the underlying, long-standing internal rot that results in the kind of domestic turmoil that, twice in the twentieth century, resulted in revolution. A balanced U.S. policy of pressure and engagement is now required to prevent the long-term risk of future accident or miscalculation that could lead to a confrontation between Russia and the West. The danger is especially evident in President Putin's effort to position Russia as the greatest competitor to the world's leading power, the United States. After the crisis of 2014, we suspended our bilateral relationship with Russia and, along with European allies, imposed economic sanctions. But our actions were insufficient to deter Russian malign influence and aggression, and now we face a bolder, more audacious Russia, willing to attack the United States directly. Russia has been weakened, but the cost of attacking the West has not been sufficiently high to prevent escalating and more frequent attacks.

Even so, the long-range U.S. goal remains a normalized relationship with Russia. Pressure must therefore be balanced with engagement, to clearly communicate the interests that the U.S. will protect and to leave open the possibility of better bilateral relations.

Russia's goal, by contrast, has been to use its hybrid approach—traditional warfare, cyberwarfare, propaganda, and more—in an effort to undermine core Western institutions and erode confidence in democracy itself. Interference in U.S. elections is only one of many means to that end. If the United States is to keep its eyes on the long-range prize of inducing Russia to become a more positive player on the global stage, and create a better balance of power, we need to be realistic in assessing Russia's reflex for threats and intimidation and its keen understanding of the divisions within our own country. When asserting power is appropriate and potentially beneficial to that long-range goal, we must learn not to self-deter in asserting it.

Such clarity of purpose is by no means easy to achieve. In September 2015, just as I came to the Joint Chiefs, Russia made an abrupt decision related to its self-promotion as chief global opponent to the United States and intervened in Syria.

That situation, suddenly altering the course of the war there, gave the United States some very specific problems, and I began my job at Joint staff diving into them. In Syria, Russian and U.S. troops were operating in the same theater—not by proxy but directly, with boots on the ground and wings in the air. Nothing like that had happened since the occupation of Germany after World War II—and back then we were allies. Close, direct involvement by the two superpowers in the same arena had rarely been a feature of the Cold War. When the United States encountered Russia in Korea and Vietnam, the Russians were masquerading as the indigenous military. Now, in Syria, they were openly carrying out military operations.

There was a volatile imbalance in the two countries' goals in the region. U.S. involvement in Syria was limited, with a short-term goal: fighting the Islamic State while implicitly supporting the Syrians, who were demanding regime change against the brutality of President Bashar al-Assad. Russia was taking a categorically different approach, entering Syria in support of the Assad regime, with a long-range goal of asserting influence in the Mideast and obstructing U.S. goals globally.

Russia's actions, therefore, were raising the stakes to a degree that posed significant challenges for us. It wasn't our policy to match the intensity of a full-on, long-term Russian commitment in Syria, so the situation quickly grew precariously out of balance. While not at war with each other, the United States and Russia were directly involved in combat in a claustrophobic space, with incompatible goals, and at disproportionate levels of commitment. As if that weren't risky enough, Russia and the United States did have one shared desire in Syria: to combat terrorist activities there by the group calling itself Islamic State of Iraq and the Levant (ISIL). This joint U.S.-Russian effort against ISIL required some collaboration between our two militaries. It necessitated forming a means to "de-conflict" the two states' operations while serving each state's interests. And yet Russia seemed to be using even our collaborations of convenience against ISIL to throw the United States off balance.

At the Pentagon, a reserve colonel was ahead of me at Joint staff, filling the assignment I was scheduled to take. So I began my work as an operations officer for the 24/7 National Military Command Center; then, when the colonel retired in November 2015, I was promoted to lieutenant colonel and started my real job. It was multifaceted. I had to analyze the U.S. approach to competing with and defeating Russia across the spectrum of conflict; put together and lead dialogue among the cross-functional, cross-departmental expert teams required to develop a military strategy in the dicey immediate geopolitical situation; write the strategy; and put it into effect, with close attention paid to the long-term goals of the United States for its relationship with Russia and for Russia's relationship with the rest of the world.

These are the kinds of highly complex, interlinked operations— delicate yet powerful—that require high regard for the professionalism and sophistication of the best-informed people. In coordinating our Russia strategy and putting it into operation, I got to know and understand the invaluable resources, in the form of brilliant, diligent experts, that the United States has at its disposal.

In November 2016, when Donald Trump won the presidential election, we at Joint were in full-on pursuit and development of Russia policy. Despite certain public statements the president had made during the campaign regarding Russia and President Putin, the incoming administration was expressing no obvious change in that policy. We in the military and foreign policy community had yet to learn how little President Trump would focus on developing any cogent policy at all, but both the outgoing Obama administration and the incoming Trump administration evidently believed in U.S.-Russian cooperation in fighting ISIL in Syria and in otherwise competing with great power rivals around the world.

But it was already becoming clear to me and to the other experts on our team that Russia had seized the initiative in Syria, which had resulted in a steady loss of U.S. influence. Under the pressure of the immediate Syria situation, and amid the threat posed by ISIL, the long view held by the United States was being set aside. We just weren't about to get into a direct fight with Russia in Syria. And the obviousness of that reality had an unfortunate tendency to encourage rather than deter Russia's pursuit of its goals there. For me, that tension posed operational challenges on a whole new level. Because its objective was dominance, Russia seemed to me more sophisticated than we were in manipulating situations for its own ends.

On the heels of coauthoring the strategy, I was also tasked with authoring a full-scale, cross-departmental plan covering all our short- and long-term military policies on Russia and a "global campaign plan" to put the strategy into operation. Coming up with such a document, and then putting it into operation, would be a massive task, requiring input from every expert at Joint staff and at multiple levels, both civilian and military, and across all branches of the armed services.

With the encouragement of my superiors, I began that process. I authored the document and coordinated the global campaign plan that would make it operational. It was an exhausting yet thrilling experience. In long days at the office, I gathered massive amounts of research, digested it, wrote draft chunks of the ultimate document, sent my writing out for review, revised it to incorporate other experts' further input, and worked all the revised chunks together into a cogent whole. We delved into how Russia fights, its psychology, its use of hybrid warfare, and its long- and short-term goals and likely behaviors. The result was to game out management of all U.S. military relationships and interactions with Russia across our entire military enterprise and across the spectrum of conflict, from competition short of armed conflict to full-scale war and everything in between. I also had the privilege of working with talented colleagues tackling similarly challenging problem sets. Those efforts allowed me to delve into the exciting arena of great power competition.

Even as we were working on the document, my ideas were percolating upward, to the top decision makers of U.S. Russia policy. That's what I mean by flying high and diving deep. And when I was asked to put together one of the regular meetings in which the chairman convenes the chiefs of service to sit down in the JCS conference room and thrash out the biggest national security issues of the moment, I got invited into a room I hadn't expected to find myself in. We call these meetings "Tanks," for the room where they happen, "the Tank." During World War II, when the Joint Chiefs was a new organization, it met with Allied British counterparts in a basement room with an arched doorway in a building on Constitution Avenue. People said entering that room was like getting into a tank.

The room has changed—it's now room 2E924 of the Pentagon, windowless and secure—but the term still holds. It's really a small boardroom: oak table, leather armchairs. For military officers, the Tank has a kind of hallowed quality. On one wall, there's a painting of President Lincoln meeting with Lt. Gen. Ulysses S. Grant, Maj. Gen. William Tecumseh Sherman, and Rear Adm. David Dixon Porter, during the Civil War. Tanks are for four-star officers, and I was a lieutenant colonel. Yet there I was, not just in the room but the person who had orchestrated the endeavor.

My strategic and operational work found its way even further upward, all the way to the awe-inspiring "warrior monk" himself: General Mattis, President Trump's first appointee as secretary of defense. I received a copy of the strategy back from Secretary Mattis with his markups on it. The completed plan influenced even bigger policy decisions. Soon, I was asked to brief highly placed members of the National Security Council, the top body for security policy. This brought me to the attention of Fiona Hill, then serving at NSC as deputy assistant to the president and senior director for European and Russian affairs. I would soon be tapped for the ultimate policy assignment: working for Director Hill at NSC.

Even as I was immersed in developing this U.S. global campaign for coping with Russia, the Syria situation was ongoing. The most immediate operational aspect of my job thus became the tricky matter of what we call "deconfliction." Given the U.S. and Russian militaries' operating in the same hot zone, sometimes collaboratively but more often not, the last thing we wanted—and the very last thing Russia wanted—was for the two militaries to find themselves maneuvering into a direct conflict with each other: the United States versus Russia in an outright battle, with the possibility for casualties on both sides. Such a situation would have explosive consequences.

And so, for the first time ever, the United States and Russia established deconfliction cells at the tactical, operational, and strategic levels. At the tactical level, these were operations centers manned 24/7. At the operational and strategic levels—my levels—these were 24/7 hotlines between the chairman of the Joint Chiefs of Staff, my top boss, Gen. Joseph Dunford, and the Russian chief of the General Staff, Valery Gerasimov. For a while, a civilian line was operational, too, between the Defense Department and the Russian Ministry of Defense, yet the major responsibility for deconfliction rested with the two militaries themselves, operating in real time. Should something slip—should our two countries' unaligned activities draw us inadvertently into a direct conflict likely to escalate on the ground—the highest-up military people on both sides could speak right away to clarify positions, bring the bigger picture into view, and, it was hoped, de-escalate.

My role in the deconfliction cell was to keep a constant eye on strategy and to provide operational support for understanding, in the most nuanced way possible, what was going on with the Russians; others on the team provided the deconfliction cell with Middle East expertise. One critical episode under my purview occurred on April 4, 2017, when Syria used chemical weapons. In response, the United States planned an air strike on a Syrian base.

The problem, from the point of view of deconfliction: Russia was occupying that very base. In the event of a U.S. strike, the Russians on the ground likely would respond. There might be casualties on both sides. Chairman Dunford fully understood the seriousness of the situation. When I got home at the end of that day, I kept my uniform on during dinner, poised to respond if the situation blew up.

Sure enough, within the hour, I was breaking the speed limit driving back to the Pentagon. Chief of the General Staff Gerasimov, Chairman Dunford's counterpart, had initiated a deconfliction call. Soon, I was in the chairman's office, listening intently to that call. I'd been asked to translate and to offer my expert's opinion on what Gerasimov was actually saying and what he might be likely to do. Though I spoke Russian fluently, I was not a trained interpreter, and I was being asked to translate maybe the tensest conversation between two military leaders since the end of the Cold War.

I was nervous but pulled off the translation. I also learned a lot. Chief Gerasimov, in his sixties, is a strongman type, used to throwing his weight around with the Russian military and with less powerful nations. We wanted most immediately to avoid a flashpoint between the two countries—and yet during the call, we were able to hold our ground, even while keeping that goal in view. This stood in contrast to certain U.S. patterns of response to Russia: the tendency to mirror-image, to miscalculate risk, to self-deter in the face of a possible blowup.

Don't self-deter. The chairman of the Joint Chiefs didn't. The upshot was neither a blowup between the United States and Russia nor paralysis in the face of Russian talents for aggression. Here was an example, in a microcosm, of the use of strength to achieve what the United States wanted from its macro Russia strategy: de-escalation.

Something else happened during my time at Joint staff that would prove decisive both to my family life and to my future career. In 2016, Eug showed up in Washington. By now, he was a lawyer. He'd served in Iraq as a judge advocate general and had then gone on to Germany as a brigade judge advocate and then on to Fort Hood, the military's largest judicial jurisdiction, as the chief of justice. Now he'd come to the Pentagon to join the Office of the Judge Advocate General.

So Eug and I were both working at the Pentagon, he on army staff, me on Joint staff. Upon his arrival, he stayed with Rachel and me for three months. Soon, he bought a house only four doors down from ours. Our daughters, eight months apart, became inseparable. Eug and I, inseparable ourselves, and irrepressible on the Brooklyn streets, hadn't been in the same place since SUNY Binghamton. Now we were commuting to work together.

Many people refer to having a quiet inner voice. As I've written, Eug has always been an exterior manifestation of my quiet inner voice. His perception of serious issues almost always matches mine, yet the steadiness of his judgment—at a slight remove from whatever I'm getting passionately involved in—is impeccable. And now my quiet inner voice was on the scene. That would prove to be an incredibly lucky development for me. Mainly, at the time, it was awesome to be in such close proximity again.

During my time at the Pentagon, I once again learned a lot about what constitutes real leadership. I was only a lieutenant colonel, but when strong leaders see something of value in their people, regardless of their place in the hierarchy, they don't merely tolerate hearing from those people; they encourage them to speak up and even to take leading roles. I'd begun to learn this feature of leadership as early as Korea, when my possibly outlandish idea of trying a platoon maneuver was approved by General Honoré, the Ragin' Cajun, and we pulled it off. I learned it in the TOC in Iraq, too, when Maj. Omar Jones sat back and let me run the operation to capture Abu Bakar. And now I was learning it from leaders at the Pentagon like Gen. Kenneth McKenzie and Chairman Dunford and from professionals at the White House itself.

Hierarchy is critical to military performance. It's critical to science, academia, movie production, corporate commerce, and any other highly refined effort that mobilizes large numbers of people. But sometimes a position in a hierarchy doesn't reflect its value to the effort. At those times, strong leaders know it, and they act on it.

By the same token, though, strong people lower in the hierarchy, with something to say, have to learn to trust their gut and embrace the excitement, as well as the potential danger, of stepping up. At Joint staff, I was operating so far beyond what people expect of a lieutenant colonel that I wasn't immediately confident in my newly influential role.

I had to learn to see myself for what I was becoming. When we had a call with our Russian counterparts to arrange a face-to-face meeting in Helsinki between Chairman Dunford and Chief Gerasimov, I saw some "old friends" on the Russian side from my posting in Moscow. When they saw me on the Joint staff, taking part in such a high-level call, I caught their reaction, which I'd loosely translate as "Hey, this guy was that Moscow military attaché! What's *he* doing here?" Soon, they'd see me sitting two chairs down from NSA

John Bolton, and I found the submerged double take they did when they saw me so highly placed both funny and exciting.

My confidence in my own role, and in the value of sometimes breaking hierarchy, was tested on June 8, 2018, when a number of us on staff were in Helsinki in the high-stakes, face-to-face meeting we'd arranged between Chairman Dunford and Chief Gerasimov. The purpose of the meeting was to allow for direct discussion of the shared deconfliction process in Syria and a broad strategic dialogue on our respective national security interests. As usual at such meetings, the top two people, Chairman Dunford and Chief Gerasimov, sat at the conference table across from each other, flanked by their senior staff, while more junior members of the delegation like me sat in chairs along the walls. At one point in the conversation, Chairman Dunford ordered the backbench staff out to allow the higher-ups to have lunch and talk in private.

I knew they were about to leave the deconfliction topic to discuss the most delicate and strategic of issues. This was often one of the more important portions of a summit; during such discussions, the respective leaders gain a better understanding of each other. The evening before, I'd led an in-depth prep session with the chairman on Russia. Both my supervisor, a brigadier general, and a civilian expert had left it to me to do the talking. And now I felt I might be crucial to this private session.

So I had a choice to make: Do I follow the order and leave the room, or do I presume I'm included in this session, even though nothing to that effect has been said? To stay in the room would mean disobeying a direct order, potentially incurring the chairman's wrath, and being ordered out again, or worse.

I knew there was a definite risk to staying. What I didn't know was what to do.

The response of the backbenchers had been somewhat slow, and the chairman had to repeat the order to leave the room. That's serious, and the others hurried their pace. Against what I feared might be my better judgment, I forced my butt to stay on that seat.

A civilian friend had been seated a few chairs down from me. As he left, he turned back to look at me. His look said "Wow." Alone now against the wall, I found that merely staying put was like willing myself out of a plane in airborne training.

Chairman Dunford looked over at me. There was a pause. Then he introduced me directly to Chief Gerasimov, telling his Russian counterpart that I was born in Ukraine. Gerasimov, the Russian strongman, looked me over, then cracked a joke in Russian. I must be the reason, Gerasimov said, that relations between the United States and Russia were so bad. Laughter ensued, to my enormous relief.

I was then asked to contribute to the ensuing dialogue. Switching among languages, I took part in deep U.S.-Russia discussions on Ukraine at the highest military level. My risk had paid off.

Later, Scott Roenicke, a longtime Russia Team member on the Joint Staff, who had been sitting a few seats to the right of Chairman Dunford, said to me, laughing and incredulous, "I can't believe you did that!"

I could hardly believe it myself. It was an unorthodox move, counterintuitive, and I took a personal risk in making it. I was learning to recognize the reality of the situation I'd achieved. You have to know your role. Trusting your gut means relying, at once, on judgment and instinct.

In July 2018, I had my last hurrah on the Joint staff. I was going up to the top of the policy ladder: to the National Security Council. After getting back from Helsinki, I had one last staff-related activity, a briefing on great power competition. It would be chaired by General McKenzie, the director of Joint staff and, as such, a three-star guaranteed to make four. After I completed the briefing, he called me over—he knew I was leaving—and invited me to drop by his office. This was a very unusual invitation for a lieutenant colonel to receive. Of course, I took him up on it. A few days later, in his office, General McKenzie and I actually ended up chatting.

"You're nowhere near the typical lieutenant colonel," the general told me. That meant more to me than I can fully express—it still does, even after all this time and all that's happened. He said that he could tell I was going places. I accepted the judgment. I was learning from great army officers—General McKenzie, Major General (ret.) McCaffrey, Major General Jones, Brigadier General (ret.) Zwack, General Dunford, and others—to believe in myself.

But I've had the same experience with some of my civilian bosses. Good leaders like them encourage expertise, demand dialogue, and expect subordinates to express opinions. There's a high regard among military professionals (and the best professionals in any endeavor) not only for expertise and sophistication, but also for honest and forthright opinion when it's well grounded.

I was leaving for NSC. There, I would come into a direct confrontation with the ill effects—for me, but also, far more important, for our country and for the stability of the world—of a lack of regard for expertise, professionalism, experience, and, above all, honesty by key figures in the Trump administration. That confrontation would have dramatic results.

CHAPTER 8

DANGER

I can't say I wasn't warned.

I'd kept in steady touch with one of my early army mentors, Omar Jones, the operations officer who let me run the operation to capture Abu Bakar in Iraq. When I was considering going to the White House to serve on the National Security Council staff, Major General Jones connected me with two senior officers already at NSC, and one of them told me, point-blank, "This will be the most dangerous and challenging environment you've ever worked in."

He added, "including combat assignments."

This officer had had multiple deployments to both Iraq and Afghanistan, so I took his point. The danger at NSC would be of a different kind, but the landscape and the people would be just as shifting and unpredictable, the situations possibly harder for some-one like me—an infantry officer, not a political animal—to read and respond to. There was little training for the kinds of challenging situations I would now have to face. I'd risen to the top echelon of the profession, and that was exciting: working at the heart of the most sensitive global drama on behalf of the United States. The great strategic conflict between the United States and Russia, my most in-demand area of expertise, had entered a new phase, in part thanks to my work on the Joint staff. The National Security Council was the logical next step. And yet with the increased excitement and importance came increased danger. But as an infantry guy, I knew that at times there's danger simply in operating at all.

What I couldn't see clearly were the brewing domestic political schemes in which the Trump administration was even then choosing to involve itself—and how domestic political chicanery would come to involve Russia and Ukraine, the key countries under my purview for U.S. strategy and policy. That's where the danger lay for me. Not seeing it coming, I would pay a great price.

One of the things I've heard said about me, even by those sympathetic to my story, is that, like Icarus of ancient Greek mythology, who flew with feather-and-wax wings, while at NSC, I simply got too close to the sun. The analogy suggests that there might have been hubris involved in my fall from grace at NSC, after I reported the presidential misconduct I was privy to. That action led to my testifying before the House, and to further reprisals, and then to my eventual decision—the hardest fall I took—to retire from the army.

Certainly I'd risen high and fast, with growing confidence. There's no doubt, too, that at times in my life, my inclination against self-deterrence and my all-important trust in my gut have led me astray.

Trying to tough out an ankle injury in Ranger School; jumping supertanker wakes with Eug in a fourteen-foot speedboat; rolling the Humvee that necessitated Operation Cabbage Patch—confidence can be a doubled-edged sword.

But I'd matured—partly thanks to the lessons I'd learned from mistakes like those. Moreover, I don't think the Icarus reference is apt. I didn't fall because I flew too close to the sun. I fell as a result of a midair collision with something I couldn't have seen coming in a million years. Moving upward in my career of service, I couldn't see—for a long time, nobody could—the untoward, possibly even unprecedented phenomenon that I would inevitably bump into: Donald Trump's accession to the presidency of the United States. My specific assignment at NSC came to dovetail, in unpredictable ways, with the activities of a new administration arriving in office just as I'd begun to reach such great heights.

What we know now is that very shortly after I arrived at NSC, certain members of the Trump administration, including the president himself, started putting a strange political scheme into operation. This scheme had no rational relationship to the foreign policy interests of the United States. Its purpose was simply to improve the president's standing going into his 2020 reelection campaign by undermining suggestions arising from the investigation by Special Counsel Robert Mueller that Russia had interfered on Trump's behalf in the 2016 election and by smearing the likely 2020 Democratic presidential nominee, Joe Biden. For reasons that became clear only later, that plan involved creating and retailing a false narrative involving, specifically, Ukraine, our key ally in the region, the home of my ancestors, and a critical part of my job.

As the NSC point person for all things Ukraine, in carrying out my duty, I would crash smack into that false narrative, one concocted for the shabbiest of reasons and unimaginably remote from anything I was working on for high-level global U.S. strategy. On that July call, my job on behalf of the long-range security interests of the United States would collide with President Trump's short-term, nickel-and-dime electoral and political sleaze. I would have to draw on everything I'd ever learned to navigate the fallout.

None of this was clear in late 2018, when I began considering a move from the Joint staff to NSC. In November, I interviewed with Special Assistant to the President Dr. Richard Hooker, the NSC's senior director for Europe and NATO and a retired army colonel. Rich was deputy to Dr. Fiona Hill, who was serving as deputy assistant to the president and senior director for all of Europe and Russia.

Rich and I hit it off right away, and during the interview, Dr. Hill came in. We all talked for a while longer, and the upshot was the dream upshot for any job interview.

"You're hired," Fiona said. "When can you start?"

I did my own due diligence. The officer Omar Jones connected me with filled me in on what he'd gleaned from his time there. There was so much turnaround in the Trump administration, and the possibility that the administration wouldn't last two terms and that leadership in the NSC directorate was likely to move on fairly quickly. If I came in now, I might soon get offered the Hooker role or something even higher. There was every possibility I would become a senior director—equivalent to a four-star rank, a prospect I found irresistibly exciting.

To take the job at NSC, I had to complete the Joint Chiefs assignment and get the army to agree to release me. After all, you're supposed to go where the army needs you, so I let the army and the White House fight that one out. I finished at Joint staff in the summer of 2018, and Rachel, Ellie, and I went on a long-planned vacation in a rented RV for several weeks, visiting Yellowstone, Glacier, and Mount Rushmore National Parks and the Little Bighorn Battlefield and Devil's Tower National Monuments. I returned to DC refreshed, invigorated, and ready for a new challenge.

I reported to NSC in July as director for Russia. Eventually, as a result of President Trump's lack of interest in countering Russian aggression, I was asked to cover eastern Europe as well, including Moldova, Belarus, and, crucially, Ukraine—a portfolio where Dr. Hill thought I could do more good in countering Russian aggression indirectly. As part of a team of consummate foreign policy professionals, I was thrilled to be doing critical work on behalf of U.S. security interests in this most troubled, dangerous, and fascinating region. Twenty years earlier, I'd begun my military career as a platoon leader in Korea. Now, in pursuit of the passion I'd first begun to know as an officer, I'd arrived in the executive office of the president of the United States: the White House itself.

I was so excited by the work that I regularly stayed in the office until 10 or 11 p.m. It was high summer, hot as always in Washington, and whenever I emerged from the Old Executive Office Building and onto the sidewalk, I'd marvel at all the tourists walking around the White House complex. I was doing my job at the core of American government.

Even as I joined the NSC team, a presidential summit was taking place in Helsinki. Following up on the meeting I'd attended with Chairman Dunford, when the chairman met with his Russian military counterpart, General Gerasimov, Helsinki would be the first face-to-face between the new president of the United States and

President Putin: the highest-level meeting in my portfolio. This was a major opportunity to advance U.S. policy.

And yet, while the discussions seemed to go well, the two presidents' joint press conference turned out to be a debacle. Expressly rejecting the consensus views of his entire intelligence apparatus, President Trump publicly took the word of Putin, the ex-KGB officer, that Russia had not interfered in the 2016 U.S. presidential elections. This inevitably raised questions about what had been discussed in the one-on-one bilateral meeting between the presidents, attended only by them and their interpreters. I felt my stomach sink as I thought about the U.S. interpreter, whom I'd come to know, becoming the focus of public attempts to determine the content of the presidential meeting. The press tore into the news story, and as the Russia director at NSC, I had to deal with some of the blowback.

Even more important, from my nuts-and-bolts angle: the new national security advisor, John Bolton—he'd been appointed shortly before I came to NSC—was working on a follow-up meeting with his own Russian counterpart. Officials on both sides were to discuss developing, in practical terms, the initiatives outlined during the presidential summit. That meeting was to be held in Geneva, and it offered the exciting prospect that I'd soon be sitting at the big table, face-to-face with our most significant adversaries in the region.

But I had another idea as well. Critical to the global campaign strategy for Russia, which I'd led at the Joint staff, was curating our relationship with Ukraine. Ukrainian Independence Day falls on August 24, and that date seemed to me to offer a rare opportunity: if we scheduled the meeting in Geneva with the Russians for August 23, we could add Ukraine to the trip and be there for the national celebration. Having fully learned my lessons, I had no reticence about speaking up when I had something to say.

In this case, the person I had to convince was NSA Bolton. As a boss, Bolton had a knack for being hard to read. You couldn't tell what he was thinking—or even if he was listening when you spoke to him. He'd be silent, seem possibly bored; then there would come a sudden head cock, and you'd realize he was tracking everything you said. If he plays poker, he's probably good at it. In the course of my time at NSC, I had dozens of interactions with him, and I was always impressed by his grasp of complicated material, his ability to quickly consume, process, and execute. He never wanted specific talking points; all he needed to make his own points was solid, big-picture background. I also admired Bolton's tactics with what he considered a hostile press: they were counterintuitive and, I thought, clever. He was exceptionally transparent, telling the press what was going on in unusually substantial detail; they might criticize, but they couldn't say he was hiding or spinning. He was also very good with foreign counterparts. A Russia hawk with decades of policy experience, he made no bones about his desire to ensure that the United States retained the greatest possible latitude with regard to arms control. At the same time, he was a savvy political operative. He seemed to enjoy having a notable persona and being called "Ambassador."

So in the course of planning the trip to Geneva, I proposed to NSA Bolton that we add the Ukraine stop. There he could meet directly with top officials and take part in the independence celebrations. This would show U.S. support for Ukraine in a clear and dramatic way, right on the heels of his meeting with the Russian national security advisor. To my great satisfaction, he took my advice, and I got busy planning the Ukraine leg.

It was quite a trip. First, I flew by commercial airline to Geneva to meet with the Russians. Now I had my own seat at the table, two chairs down from NSA Bolton, as he and Nikolai Patrushev, secretary of the Security Council of the Russian Federation, discussed outcomes of the Helsinki face-to-face between Presidents Trump and Putin. Bolton was holding a firm and consistent line. Among other things, he advised Secretary Patrushev that the United States could not tolerate and would not accept Russia's repeating its interference in the 2016 U.S. presidential election and 2018 midterm elections; he insisted that any joint statement would have to include a reference to such interference. He also made it clear that the United States did not recognize Russia's annexation of Crimea. And he noted U.S. disapproval of any Russian interference in the intense Ukrainian election cycle, already gearing up for 2019. In the end, no joint statement was signed with the Russians.

We then flew military air to Kyiv for the meeting with top Ukraine politicians and the celebration of Ukraine's Independence Day. This was a huge highlight for me: one day Russia, next day Ukraine, the dual hotspots of my portfolio. And the national security advisor's meeting with the Ukrainians went well.

When we got back to DC, my major focus became the security of the 2019 Ukrainian elections, which were widely seen in our policy community and by our allies as pivotal for the nation and the region. The incumbent president of Ukraine, Petro Poroshenko, was facing challenges by dozens of candidates from a dizzying array of parties. A leading candidate had emerged: Volodymyr Zelensky, a comedian and actor running on a platform of reform, anticorruption, and public trust in government. There was strong potential for real improvement within Ukraine, but persistent election corruption within the country made it an obvious target for Russian interference. We had to do everything we could to ensure this election's integrity.

I proposed to NSA Bolton an action plan for securing the Ukraine election. Such plans distill all issues relevant to our policy and goals for a region, with a focus on gaming out each key activity that must occur in order to achieve certain aims, with detailed time lines within other time lines—a kind of hyperactive Gantt chart, full of milestones and dependencies. NSA Bolton approved, and I launched and coordinated a multifaceted effort that involved many meetings of many agencies and offices across the government. In that process, I began to develop strong relationships with various counterparts.

Among the key people I came to know and respect as we worked closely together was Marie "Masha" Yovanovitch, the U.S. ambassador to Ukraine. Like mine, her family had fled the Soviet Union, but in the 1950s; Masha was born in Montreal, Canada, and grew up in Connecticut. I also worked closely with Bill Taylor, the Vietnam War–era infantry officer and foreign policy professional who would replace Masha when Trump recalled her on the basis of a smear. I worked, too, with Laura Cooper, deputy assistant secretary of defense for Russia, Ukraine, and Eurasia; and with George Kent, the former deputy chief of mission to Ukraine, now the deputy assistant secretary for the State Department, with responsibility for the same countries I covered at the National Security Council; George and I would work very closely together during my nineteen months at NSC. Like me, many of these people would soon be caught up in the events surrounding presidential wrongdoing and become known to TV viewers of the 2020 impeachment hearings.

Working with such superb people, and experiencing their commitment and finesse, confirmed many of the leadership lessons

I'd been learning throughout my career. I was blown away by the professionalism, the sheer institutional expertise, that the United States had at its disposal. These people were an invaluable resource, driven by brains, experience, and integrity. Together, we gave everything we had, every day, to gain the best possible outcome for the tense, volatile region under our purview.

We were of course increasingly aware that the president's focus was decidedly not on U.S. interests or advancing U.S. policies and security. This was a subject of real concern. What we didn't know, however, was how his total focus on his own political goals would undermine the strength of the critically important national institutions we were serving.

On November 25, 2018, Russia and Ukraine, the two most important nations in my portfolio, came at direct military odds yet again. Given my role at NSC, it was now on me to provide expertise in leading an effective U.S. government response to this new display of Russian aggression. In the ensuing international crisis, I got a close look at President Trump's instincts for how to handle Russia strategy. What I saw was disappointing.

That morning, two small Ukrainian military boats and a tugboat, en route from Odessa, approached the Kerch Strait. Russia had illegally bridged the strait, giving itself direct access to Crimea after annexing it from Ukraine back in 2014. As the Ukrainian vessels came near, the Russians placed a barge in the passage of the strait, and Russian Coast Guard boats ordered the Ukrainians to submit to inspection, claiming—based on the Crimea annexation, although the annexation remains unrecognized by most of the world—that the approach was an illegal entry into Russian territorial waters.

The Ukrainians refused to leave, citing a 2003 treaty on freedom of navigation in the area. The Russian Coast Guard proceeded to fire on the Ukrainian Navy, ram the Ukrainian tug repeatedly, and then try to ram the gunboats. In the process, two Russian ships collided. The Ukrainian vessels withdrew from the strait, to international waters, aborting their lawful transit through the strait. But the Russian Coast Guard, Navy, and Air Force pursued them, and Russia started patrolling the strait by air, with fighter jets and helicopters. Pursued and fired upon, the Ukrainian ships turned and headed back to Odessa. Finally, they were captured in international waters by the Russian Coast Guard. The Russians would later charge the Ukrainian sailors with violating Russian immigration laws.

This was the first test of the Trump White House regarding a conflict between our key ally and our major opponent in the explosive part of the world under my purview. I immediately assembled the U.S. government team, and together we devised several options that would signal support for Ukraine and pushback on Russian aggression while minimizing the risks of an accident or miscalculation. I communicated the options to NSA Bolton.

Here was a classic Russian display of dominance, I advised him. The Russians were relying, as usual, on our not knowing what to do in the face of their belligerence. Russia is adept at a technique—it's part of a uniquely Russian doctrine called "reflexive control"—in which it conveys information that inclines an opponent to overreact to a risk and to self-deter, thus making the very decision Russia desires. Instead, I recommended that the United States take a strong position, both on behalf of our allies in the immediate region and in support of our own strategy for deterring Russian aggression. Bolton seemed to agree with my assessment, and I had hope for a strong U.S. response.

It was therefore an unpleasant surprise when President Trump failed his first test of U.S. resolve regarding Russia. In the end, the United States took no leadership role at all in response to the incident in the Kerch Strait. Worse yet, President Trump directed a lockdown of any military activity in the region, basically signaling U.S. weakness. Things went just as the Russians might have hoped. While Secretary of State Mike Pompeo made statements condemning the Russian action, a message echoed by U.S. officials at the United Nations, President Trump fell into a classic state of decision paralysis. He was clearly afraid that anything he did would risk triggering reprisals by Russia that he had no strategy for managing. He was not in alignment with the strategic analysis of his professional diplomatic and military community, yet he had no other analysis of his own—just a misinformed sense of the risks. He overreacted to the possible consequences of taking any action. In short, the United States self-deterred—or, so I thought at the time, but as I write this, I wonder if there was a more basic reason for the president's inaction to protect U.S. interests. It seems possible that President Trump simply didn't care about the U.S. interests and was more concerned about not upsetting President Putin.

It's true, of course, that the consequences of any direct engagement might be potentially catastrophic, but in this case, those odds were nonexistent. The error came in allowing the prospect of catastrophe to wipe out the ability to make any risk calculation at all. By overreacting and shutting down, the president took a risk—an uncalculated one. He risked overall U.S. policy paralysis regarding

Russia. This left big, important sectors of the world vulnerable to explosive events, with unpredictable consequences; it eroded Russia's fears of reprisal for attacking U.S. interests; it eroded deterrence and resulted in bounties on U.S. troops in Afghanistan and massive, unprecedented cyberattacks that did not trigger a response from President Trump; and it perpetuated the vicious circle eroding deterrence. President Trump's actions went a long way toward escalating the risk of confrontation. Eventually, the Russians will miscalculate, thinking we will stay silent—and when we do, the risk of escalation will be great.

By early 2019, Special Counsel Robert Mueller's investigation of the 2016 Trump campaign's relationship to Russia had returned a number of indictments of highly placed Trump allies and cronies and threatened to touch the president himself. In that context, Rudolph Giuliani began making moves regarding the part of the world under my purview at NSC—moves that I couldn't clearly read and didn't know what to make of.

The former mayor of New York City and the president's personal attorney, Giuliani had no foreign policy portfolio, no official role for representing U.S. interests with Ukraine. Yet according to his own public statements, he was acting as a lawyer on behalf of a client under investigation, President Trump, and as such, he appeared to be developing alternate hypotheses involving Ukraine that would, he asserted, exonerate the president of colluding with Russia during his campaign and implicate Ukraine, rather than Russia, in the 2016 presidential election interference. This, of course, was the same story the Russians had now been pushing for two years.

Giuliani said he wanted Ukrainian prosecutors to aid his own personal investigation into these allegations. And he publicly noted the involvement of Hunter Biden, the former vice president's son, in a Ukrainian company, implying corruption on the part of the Biden family. But every U.S. intelligence agency knew, and had stated, that there was nothing to these allegations, that they amounted to Russian propaganda.

To us in the policy community, Giuliani's moves were bewildering but also, at first, a lot more noise than signal. People who have read the retrospective reporting have a better sense of what was happening than I or my colleagues could have had at the time—or would necessarily have wanted to have. In early 2019, our focus at the National Security Council was not on the politics of the Mueller investigation, or the president's image going into the 2020 election, or the unusual goings-on by the large number of unusual characters around this particular president. Nothing in Giuliani's erratic statements and behavior could shift my attention away from our immediate, overarching effort: to secure the integrity of the 2019 Ukraine election. In a strange time, with many shady characters making many shady moves, it was especially important to remain professional and stay laser-focused on the policy and strategy complexities at hand.

But try as we did to compartmentalize Giuliani as a person with his own strange agenda far from the center of our policymaking work, his actions started to invade our institutional spaces, with the effect of undermining U.S. foreign policy interests. In March, negative stories began circulating about the U.S. ambassador to Ukraine, Masha Yovanovitch, with whom I'd been working on securing the upcoming election. Giuliani was a purveyor of some of these baseless reports about Ambassador Yovanovitch, but it wasn't just him: John Solomon, a conservative commentator for the website The Hill, had clearly been fed false information about Masha, and he began publishing it.

The germ of the slander seemed to have come from Ukraine's prosecutor-general, Yuriy Lutsenko, a man well known to us as deeply corrupt. Lutsenko made the audacious and spurious claim that it was Masha Yovanovitch who was conspiring to shut down anticorruption efforts in Ukraine. He even said that she'd pressured him personally to give certain bad actors a pass and had presented him with a "do not prosecute" list. (Lutsenko would later recant this falsehood.)

I did my best to try to get NSC to go out on a limb to support Ambassador Yovanovitch, who, as far as I and the other professionals were concerned, was doing a terrific job. But the president's son Donald Trump Jr. approvingly tweeted a Daily Wire article repeating the slanderous claims, and then President Trump began repeating them publicly. At the end of April, the president directed Secretary Pompeo to recall Ambassador Yovanovitch.

For the United States to recall an ambassador at the behest, essentially, of a corrupt official of that ambassador's host country, in league with unofficial U.S. actors—this was unprecedented, the kind of thing only weak countries are sometimes forced to do in their diplomatic relationships. Masha's recall had the effect of further bewildering us at NSC and across the foreign policy community. The immediate result seemed to be to remove some impediments to whatever Giuliani was trying to get going in Ukraine.

On April 21, 2019, amid this increasingly unhappy and confused series of events, the runoff election was held in Ukraine. Confident that Zelensky would win, I had put together in advance of the election a "call package" for President Trump, which included details on the emerging post-election situation in Ukraine and talking points for him to use when congratulating Zelensky. The package was in line with the larger, painstakingly developed U.S. strategy regarding Ukraine, Russia, and eastern Europe. I wrote up a memo to the president covering all this. NSA Bolton approved that memo and reviewed the package and talking points for the president. Zelensky won by a landslide, and on a flight back to Washington from Florida, President Trump called him.

As I listened to their call, I was pleased. The mood was very good. The president used most of the talking points—a win. President-elect Zelensky asked for a bilateral meeting and invited the president to his inauguration. Despite the troubling recent events regarding Ukraine, the situation seemed potentially encouraging.

Three days later, Joe Biden officially entered the Democratic primaries for the 2020 presidential election.

I didn't spend a lot of time thinking about ongoing electoral politics at home. The immediate daily facts for me, in late April and into the summer, remained highly practical, totally and sometimes exhaustingly absorbing, and focused on the international situation. There were the normal bilateral relationships to manage with all my portfolio countries, and we had to find ways to encourage the president not to destabilize our relationship with Ukraine. With President Zelensky now on the scene, we at the National Security Council and the State Department were doubling down on cooperating on reform and anticorruption efforts in Ukraine.

So on my own initiative and with my bosses' buy-in, I put together another action plan, this time for securing the integrity of other elections in the region, though with eyes always especially on

Ukraine. It proved a monumental, months-long effort in which I chaired many meetings held in the White House conference rooms or sat beside Fiona Hill while she chaired them. The stakes were high. I was especially focused on progress on energy sector reform and achieving some successes in energy sector cooperation. Another major initiative was fostering multilateralism among Ukraine, Poland, and other regional players. There was an ongoing, related issue: China had been trying to acquire Motor Sich, Ukraine's premier aircraft engine manufacturer, and the U.S. government was making a full-court press to prevent Beijing from using corruption to acquire the company and its advanced technologies.

These endlessly complex, longer-range issues required a lot of work. There certainly wasn't any time for speculation regarding politics. But politics kept cropping up. President Zelensky's inauguration was scheduled for May 20, and the White House planned to send Vice President Mike Pence to attend. But then things started getting really strange. In early May, Giuliani redoubled his efforts and started very publicly talking down Ukraine. He told reporters that he would personally be traveling to Kyiv and that he hoped to meet with President-elect Zelensky to ask him personally to pursue certain investigations of interest to President Trump. Giuliani reiterated his baseless allegation that shifted the blame for interference in the 2016 U.S. election away from Russia and toward Ukraine. And at NSC, Director Hill said that President Trump had ordered Vice President Pence not to attend Zelensky's inauguration after all. This was a stark decision, one that seemed designed to send a deliberately negative message to President Zelensky.

Ambassador Bolton sent me to the Zelensky inauguration. In my long career trajectory, and in the far longer trajectory of my family in Ukraine and the United States, that inauguration trip was momentous. Arriving in the home of my ancestors, I was representing the White House—the center of all U.S. diplomatic and military power. It was a long way from my family's arrival in New York City on Christmas Day 1979, in flight from Soviet tyranny, with only $759, some suitcases, and my dad's intense commitment to a better life for us.

The inauguration of President Zelensky celebrated an event with potential import for changing the entire future of the region. It was possible—and it remains possible—to imagine a new direction for Ukraine, on the model of Poland in the 1990s and 2000s: a more democratic and reformed country, its endemic corruption in check, a member of the European Union. During that inauguration trip, I had meetings with the "princes"-to-be of the incoming Zelensky administration, upstarts new to high-risk politics, domestic or international; and I met on my own with various senior officials.

And I met with President Zelensky himself, who struck me as very smart and thoughtful. He was also funny—as a comedian should be—yet in no way superficial. With the recent Giuliani shenanigans in mind, I had something specific to communicate to the new president of Ukraine. I cautioned him, directly, to do everything he could to keep from getting drawn into domestic U.S. political wrangling. There, only danger lay. Coming from me, and aligned with the thinking of NSA Bolton, my advice represented the official advice of the United States.

Cocking his head to the side, Zelensky gave me a quizzical look. He might have been wondering why this low-level staffer was lecturing him. Or, more likely, he might have been taking my remarks as wise counsel, coming from Bolton and the United States and aligned with his own thinking, yet in conflict with the advice and pressure he was getting from Giuliani.

I also participated, as the White House representative, in a ceremony of the fallen that commemorated those who had died in the recent fighting with Russia. I was invited to visit the Hall of Heroes and to meet the grieving families—mothers, sisters, and young children of Ukraine's dead—laying flowers at the marker memorializing their sacrifice.

And I visited my mother's grave site and cleaned it up.

I had one other, rather strange meeting during that trip. This was with Oleksandr Danyliuk, the head of Ukraine's National Security Council and a man my own age. Danyliuk had been Ukraine's minister of finance. He and I had met before, in Washington. Fiona Hill had been away, so I took the meeting, during which Danyliuk and I discovered that we'd lived in the same apartment building in Kyiv as very small kids; we'd probably played together as toddlers.

Now, as we discussed the staffing needs of the various ministries and the need for experienced, competent, and reform-minded people, Danyliuk, with a slight smirk on his face, offered me a job in the incoming Zelensky administration. Not just any job, but a big job: defense minister for Ukraine, a post parallel to our secretary of defense.

I was surprised. While it's true that certain countries seek out U.S. talent and regional expertise, and while I did have the Ukrainian diaspora connection, as a forty-four-year-old U.S. Army lieutenant colonel, I was rather young and relatively low-ranked for such an important post. I couldn't tell if he was serious, but after I turned him down, Danyliuk repeated the offer, and then repeated it again, so I began to realize that he was serious. I'd heard of one fellow foreign area officer who had received a similar invitation and had accepted it. I duly documented the offer and reported it, as appropriate, to Fiona Hill and NSC security.

Later, when I was testifying before the House, minority counsel Stephen Castor asked me about it. The White House henchmen must have screened all my emails, looking desperately for something compromising. That job offer was all they could come up with, and they found it only because I had reported it. It was a nonissue for the counterintelligence community, and I found it surprising—even amusing.

The most troubling aspect of the whole incident was that the White House took a document I had classified as confidential and leaked it to Republicans looking to discredit me. If I hadn't already been extremely cautious, and conscious of the dangers around me, that little episode would have gotten me there.

Back home, straight from the heights of the trip in Ukraine, I crashed into a rapidly developing calamity for U.S. policy in the region.

Rudolph Giuliani's false narratives about Ukraine had started to blow up. The president himself was repeating them, telling people in the White House that the Ukrainians had tried to destroy him in the 2016 election. He even referred to a bizarre allegation that the 2016 breach of the Democratic National Committee computer network—a hack clearly perpetrated by Russia—had actually been carried out by certain actors in Ukraine, with a supposedly missing DNC server involved in a mysterious cover-up.

These made-for-TV conspiracy dramas were undermining our painstakingly developed U.S. policy consensus and the Congress's own bipartisan agenda: full support for Ukraine as a matter of vital national security. Fiona Hill was trying to manage a situation that was spiraling into crisis.

I recommended to Fiona and NSA Bolton that NSC debrief President Trump directly regarding the recent Ukraine trip. As the NSC expert on the region, I thought I could give the president my sense of the realities of the situation there and try to dispel the destructive fantasies being spun by Giuliani and others. My bosses declined the idea of an NSC debrief, thinking it risky and futile. Instead, through Mick Mulvaney, the White House chief of staff, Gordon Sondland, the ambassador to the European Union, organized a debrief to President Trump on Ukraine to which I was invited.

I looked forward to the opportunity of an Oval Office meeting, even as we still didn't have a clear understanding of the shifting political terrain or where the oddball attacks on Ukraine were coming from, or to what end. Yet when it became apparent that Sondland and Mulvaney were themselves somehow connected to the Giuliani operation, my higher-ups saw potential danger in my being out front expressing dissent from a narrative whose authors and purposes we couldn't yet track. My bosses and I feared that if whatever was going on turned into something scandalous, I'd be a witness to it, and could later get hauled into Congress to testify.

I thus found myself in a funny position: I'd received an official invitation to the Oval Office for a meeting with the president, and I declined it. These days, I like to tell people that I was invited to meet President Trump but decided I had better things to do.

My bosses' protective instincts were good ones. Sen. Ron Johnson, a staunch supporter of Ukraine, but a stauncher Trump ally, was at the Sondland debrief. Later, preceding me in testifying before the House, he would be highly critical of me. It would turn out that a network of people around the president, including Republicans in the legislative branch, were working on promoting these specious anti-Ukraine allegations. These backroom machinations were more extensive than I could know at the time, and their cast of characters, according to reports by the media, included Rep. Devin Nunes, who, as ranking member of the House Intelligence Committee, would lead the questioning in the impeachment hearings.

Yet I still thought my expertise on the real issues, when clearly communicated, might help turn the tide of whatever catastrophe was being unleashed. The way I saw it, this was the United States—not the Soviet Union, whose corrupt systems of reprisal my family had fled back in the 1970s. I felt safe enough—and, in the old infantry sense, I still wanted to be forward enough—to get in there and put things right. I now think that when it came to the potentially cutthroat realities of partisan politics and even of inter- and intraoffice relationships, Fiona saw me as somewhat naïve. I was looking to dive in and get a job done. She was trying to keep me out of the danger about which I'd been warned.

Amid all this, we were still just trying to do our jobs, now somewhat desperately, against a host of mounting obstacles. With the recall of Masha Yovanovitch from Ukraine, the canceled Pence trip to the Zelensky inauguration, and all the fantastical talk coming from Giuliani and the president, what we were really doing every day, both at NSC and the other agencies with responsibility for a potentially explosive situation, was undoing the damage being caused by our own White House, and by the president of the United States himself, and collaborating to get the U.S. relationship with Ukraine back on track.

There still seemed to be some potential. Ukraine needed us, and we and our allies needed Ukraine. The president's congratulatory April call to Zelensky had gone well, and we thought it might have given us something to build on . . .

Then the hammer fell.

Even as Giuliani's tales about Ukraine proliferated, certain White House inquiries into military aid to Ukraine began to emerge. Then, on Wednesday, July 3, an order came from the White House: Place a hold on U.S. security assistance to Ukraine.

This was a disaster for Ukraine and for all U.S. policy in the region. The security assistance was nearly four hundred million dollars, earmarked by Congress and critical to Ukraine's ability to deter Russian aggression in eastern Europe. The Trump administration had primarily an implementation role in passing the assistance to Ukraine—doing anything more risked running afoul of the Impoundment Control Act of 1974. Earlier, we'd received some general questions from the president's people regarding the security aid: How much was it? How was it spent? While this was odd, such inquiries weren't entirely untoward. This hold, however, was beyond the pale. It was in absolute opposition to the confirmed policy of the United States and our regional allies and to the consensus of all U.S. professional institutions accountable for the region. Overnight, our ally Ukraine, and therefore all of eastern Europe, faced enhanced danger from Russia.

Even stranger: the White House Office of Management and Budget had placed the hold, ostensibly, to ensure that the funding remained aligned with administration priorities. This was highly unusual, and well outside OMB's purview. Clearly, Mulvaney—still serving as director for OMB while also serving as White House chief of staff—was behind it. I couldn't connect all the dots, and I didn't have time, anyway. The full-blown crisis now fully upon us had clearly been caused by people around the president, obviously including Giuliani, but that wasn't the main concern. This was an *emergency*.

Suddenly, we were working around the clock to get the hold reversed and avoid disaster. Fulfilling my role as interagency orchestrator, I led this process, convening a Sub-Policy Coordination Committee to get the whole community of interest on Ukraine together. By July 21, this would become a higher-level meeting, a full PCC. On the twenty-third, I would coordinate yet another PCC. Meanwhile, attorneys at Defense, Justice, and State were looking at the legality of the hold: Congress had approved the aid. Scrambling, on almost no sleep and with no time for our families, we began to feel that we might be getting somewhere. We were arriving at a strong recommendation to reverse the hold and a demand for legal accountability from OMB.

Then, on the tenth, in the midst of this all-out effort, there was a further nausea-inducing development, and another as-yet-unconnected dot came into view.

Oleksandr Danyliuk, the head of Ukraine's NSC—the man who had offered me the job as Ukraine's defense minister during my recent trip there—visited the White House for a series of meetings. It was his first trip to Washington as the Ukraine national security advisor, and he arrived with specific proposals for Ukraine-U.S. cooperation that were well in keeping with the action plan we'd been developing. I had a series of engagements with Danyliuk during his visit, including a meeting with retired lieutenant general Joseph Keith Kellogg, Vice President Pence's national security advisor, and a meeting with Fiona Hill. Then, on July 10, there was a big meeting in Bolton's office to allow Danyliuk to present his plan.

Bolton had a nice corner office, but it wasn't very big, so it was a full house. The table seated only eight. Bolton generally didn't like extra people at meetings, but I'd wanted certain people there—especially Kurt Volker, the U.S. special representative for Ukraine

With my twin brother, Eugene *(left)*; Kyiv, 1977

My mother, Nona; circa 1965

The three Vindman brothers—
me and Eugene *(left)* with our
older brother, Leonid; Kyiv, 1978

My brothers and me making bear claws, with our father,
Semyon; Brooklyn, 1981 *(Credit: Carol Kitman)*

A preschool portrait
(I'm on the right);
New York City, 1981

Exploring New York City; circa 1981
(Credit: Carol Kitman)

Our first family vacation with our "new mom,"
Lyudmila ("Mila"); circa 1984

My best friend, Victor Olshansky, and me during a field exercise; Korea, 2000

At my ranger school graduation with my brother and then Brigadier General and Deputy Commanding General of the Infantry School, Lieutenant General Benjamin Freakley; September 2003

At my Purple Heart
award ceremony; Iraq,
October 2004

Eugene and me at my promotion to lieutenant colonel, in the
Joint Staff Flag Room of the Pentagon; November 2015

With my wife, Rachel, and my daughter, Eleanor, at the top
of Bunsen Peak; Yellowstone, June 2018

My family at the
White House Easter
Egg Roll; April 2019

The US delegation sent to the inauguration of Ukrainian president
Volodymyr Zelensky; May 2019

Touring the West
Wing with our father;
September 2019

At a family wedding in
September 2019.
As soon as we returned
home on the following day,
our lives were
irretrievably changed.

Submitting my
retirement request;
July 8, 2020

negotiations—and Bolton seemed to be handling the unusual size of the crowd pretty well. At the table with him sat Danyliuk and his delegation, along with Volker, Ambassador Sondland, and the U.S. energy secretary, Rick Perry. Fiona, and I, along with an NSA energy official, were backbenching, just off the table.

I scribbled notes as Danyliuk presented Bolton with a set of highly coherent proposals for cooperation. He was keeping it "big picture"—just the kind of thing Bolton liked. Everything seemed to me to be going well. *This meeting just might*, I thought, *have a powerful effect on getting a key relationship back in line with U.S. policy consensus.*

Then something strange happened. The discussion came back around to the big Ukrainian ask: a meeting between President Zelensky and President Trump—and Bolton abruptly ended the meeting. I was still catching up on my notes and, with the sudden dismissal, didn't immediately connect what I'd heard—Sondland's suggestion that in order to get a meeting with President Trump, Zelensky should undertake investigations into the Bidens. As I left the room with the others, I was still thinking the meeting had gone pretty well, that Bolton had taken what he needed from it and dismissed us all. He could be that brusque, so an abrupt dismissal wasn't all that alarming.

After a brief photo op with the Ukrainians outside the West Wing, I went straight into a "next steps" meeting with all the same people—absent Bolton—and now I heard it all clearly. There, Sondland forthrightly proposed a quid pro quo to Danyliuk: if Ukraine made a series of investigations into the 2016 election, he said, focusing on the roles of the Bidens in Ukraine and Burisma, the company on whose board Hunter Biden had served, then a bilateral meeting would be arranged. Sondland was clearly expecting Ukraine to conduct a public investigation tarnishing the Bidens and arming the administration with a way to discredit Trump's likely opponent in the 2020 presidential election.

Speaking for NSC, I directly and passionately objected to this deal. I knew, I told Sondland, that everyone wanted to get the relationship with Ukraine on track, but this was by no means the way to do it. I also told him that NSC would not be a party to the venture, and that I thought his statements were inappropriate. Investigating the Bidens had nothing to do with national security; this kind of thing was certainly nothing that we, at NSC, were about to get involved in. Then Fiona Hill came in, and she backed me up.

In the face of our rejection, Sondland seemed prepared to back off. But his proposal was an unsettling eye-opener. Those of us at NSC, and in the whole policy community for eastern Europe, now knew something we hadn't known before: All the Ukraine interference clearly wasn't just some wackadoodle scheme run by Rudolph Giuliani for political reasons of his own. There were government officials like Sondland involved—and the policy community, it became apparent that day, was in direct, open conflict with them.

As we walked out of the West Wing, Fiona filled me in on what I'd missed. When he'd heard Sondland suggest that Zelensky would get his meeting once he undertook an investigation into Joe and Hunter Biden, Bolton had suddenly stiffened and sat upright. It was this improper suggestion that had led him to end the meeting so abruptly, and to pull Fiona aside to warn her off supporting what he called Sondland's and Mulvaney's "drug deal."

Meanwhile, in Kyiv, President Zelensky dissolved the Parliament and called for new elections, scheduled for July 21. In these, his reform party enjoyed an unprecedented landslide—the kind of overwhelming party victory that parliamentary systems almost never see. That outcome seemed to offer us an ideal opportunity to revive the upbeat mood of the president's congratulatory call of April, back when Zelensky himself had won.

The president agreed to participate in another congratulatory call, but then Bolton rejected the idea. I was disappointed, but at the time, we were mostly consumed with getting the hold on the security funds reversed. Then, surprisingly, the call was back on. None of this seesawing made any sense. The call, supposedly to congratulate Zelensky on the election results, had now been delayed for several days after the Ukraine elections. With Sondland's actions from a few weeks earlier in mind, I feared the worst with regard to what was really going on and what might happen on the call. Still, I clung to the hope that the call could help get things back on track.

I got going on writing up the talking points. The call was scheduled for 9 a.m. on July 25. We were to listen in from the smaller of the two Situation Rooms in the basement of the West Wing.

CHAPTER 9

THE ABSENCE OF THE NORMAL

If what I just heard becomes public," I told Eug, "the president will be impeached."

It was July 25, 2019. I'd just returned from the White House Situation Room to the third floor of the Old Executive Office Building, where Eug and I had our offices at NSC. I'd come straight into Eug's office.

I meant what I told him—but I didn't expect the president to be impeached. And I didn't expect what I'd heard on the call to become public.

What I expected, when I showed up in my brother's office—still trying to process the enormity of what President Trump had said on the call with President Zelensky—was simply to report what I'd heard to the appropriate people. While I knew that others in the White House basement had heard what I'd heard, I didn't think anyone else was going to do anything about it.

In any case, I was the director for Ukraine. I had the responsibility here. If I didn't report what I knew up the chain of command, no one might ever know that the president had subverted the established foreign policy of the United States for his own benefit in an upcoming election.

That's why I was standing in my brother's office. From the moment I heard the president say, "Do us a favor, though," and then ask for a Ukrainian government investigation into former vice president Joe Biden and his son Hunter, I knew it was totally improper: certainly awful and possibly unlawful. I also sensed right away that my immediate boss, Tim Morrison, Fiona Hill's recent replacement, had no intention of responding in any way to this gross impropriety (or illegality, for all I knew), but would simply blow off the conversation. Everything I'd ever learned, from my ancestry, in my family life, and throughout my career—decisiveness under pressure, courage, honesty, always being forthright, knowing where you are and what your role is, speaking up—made it overwhelmingly obvious to me that I had no other choice. Regardless of any impact on the president, on government institutions, or on myself, I had to report what I'd heard. The duty to report misconduct is a critical component of U.S. Army leadership, as well as of the oath I'd taken to the U.S. Constitution. Despite the president's constitutional role as commander in chief, the head of the military that I had spent decades serving—in fact, *because* of his role—I had an obligation to report what he'd done. My duty was clear, and I would do my duty, as I always had, to the best of my ability.

That part was simple. The next steps were complicated. Doing the right thing means doing the right thing in the right way, and that by no means included making public what I'd heard the president say. My duty was simply to report the truth up the chain of command.

In the ensuing weeks and months, I would fill in the remaining gaps in my understanding of the Ukraine extortion scheme: the strange behavior of Giuliani in Ukraine, the inappropriate quid pro quo that Sondland had offered Ukrainian officials, the president's own flagrant wrongdoing. But I couldn't have connected the dots that day. I was still reacting to a moment, an action, that debased the office of the president.

I was also quickly shifting into crisis management mode. After what had already been a long, enervating, overtime effort throughout the spring and summer, there was now an even greater need to manage and reset the chaos that the president's people were causing for the United States. U.S. policy for eastern Europe and Russia—my NSC portfolio, all-important to U.S. security interests—had been tottering throughout the spring and summer. Now, after the call, it lay in pieces. That was my whole focus.

So my first thought was that the president's breach, like everything else that had gone so disastrously wrong, could be, must be, managed and corrected; that, as had occurred so many times before, he could be convinced to reverse his decision. Once the responsible people up the chain of command, the people with the proper clearances and need to know, learned of the president's actions, we in the broader policy community could act. We could figure out how to advise the president on his gross error in judgment, walk back and cancel his inappropriate demand, and continue to move toward stabilizing relationships and executing a cogent foreign policy. If it was my duty to report the president's misconduct, then it was our collective duty to assess the damage, manage the fallout, have the wayward president's most senior counselors rein him in, and get our jobs done. That was the process I planned to start.

From behind his desk, Eug was looking at me, disconcerted. As I relayed everything I'd just heard, my brother didn't ask many questions, didn't question my interpretation of the facts—we didn't even discuss the risks of reporting my concerns. Such was our bond that Eug and I could read the moral situation, and my moral obligation, at a glance. He simply agreed, without any hesitation, that I had a duty to report the disastrous impropriety I'd heard and see if more senior White House authorities could rectify the situation. While I didn't yet know that the ground was shifting beneath my feet, or that my life was changing for good, I was already feeling incredibly lucky that my twin—my quiet inner voice—was also the chief NSC ethics officer, a highly experienced lawyer with all the right security clearances.

Doing the right thing the right way meant reporting the wrongdoing to Eug's boss, the senior attorney at NSC, John Eisenberg. My own boss Tim Morrison had not only heard the call himself but had also blown off my suggestion that we ask legal to listen in. And when hearing the president demand the investigation of the Bidens, Tim had seemed, at first, quite surprised, then resigned, just moving on. Unlike Fiona, Tim is a purely political animal, transactional and defensive, with little expertise in or concern for the region in our purview. He would shut down anything he saw as rocking his own boat. There was little point in further discussing the call with him. I had to take it to Eisenberg.

I tested my feelings about Tim that same day, asking him, point-blank, the critical question: "Are we supposed to do anything with this call? Is this a change of policy?" I asked. With a wave of his hand and a smirk, again he dismissed the whole issue. What we'd heard on the call was nothing more, to him, than one more frustrating Trump tangent—nothing to see here, nothing to talk about. But I knew he understood the degree to which crucial U.S. foreign policy was being held hostage by some sleazy domestic political consideration. Indeed, his and my views on the Ukraine crisis were aligned. Tim was excellent at manipulating the bureaucracy to achieve his aims. I trusted that he would take steps to reverse the hold on security assistance, but I knew he wouldn't do anything about the call.

Eug and I went together to report the call to John Eisenberg. I was beginning a process in which I expected the appropriate professionals to sort things out and correct a situation that was disastrous for the country and, potentially, the globe. The process didn't go the way I expected.

My meeting with Eisenberg was brief. I told him what I'd heard the president demand and that I was sure it was wrong. Impassive, Eisenberg wrote down what I said on a yellow legal pad. He asked me if I thought I had heard something criminal. This seemed a strange question. I replied that I couldn't make that kind of determination; I only knew that it was improper. I was already sensing that he was managing me. It would soon become clear that, while a sharp attorney, Eisenberg is all about saving his own skin. Acting on this report I was making would put him at odds with the president.

Eisenberg then called in his deputy, Michael Ellis, to discuss how best to handle the matter. The call hadn't been recorded. There was a transcript, however, and Eisenberg and Ellis began discussing in front of me how to store it.

Normally, the transcripts for such calls are stored on a server to which relevant officials at NSC have access. But there's also a server dedicated to deeply secret information, with very limited access. Usually, this latter server holds files regarding covert operations and other intelligence matters; calls with foreign leaders don't get stored there.

But now a routine congratulatory call had turned into something highly sensitive, and Eisenberg was talking about placing the transcript on the secret server, where few would ever be able to find it. If there was nothing wrong with the call, this would be an unusual and strange thing to do. The secret server is explicitly not to be used for concealing violations of law, inefficiency, or administrative error, or preventing embarrassment to a person, organization, or agency. I suggested filing the transcript in the normal fashion, but now Eisenberg wasn't listening to me. The transcript of the call would be buried.

Several days later, I reviewed that transcript, as reconstructed by the White House communications staff. Missing were both President Trump's words saying that Joe Biden had been recorded discussing Ukraine corruption and President Zelensky's words explicitly mentioning Burisma Holdings, the energy company on whose board Hunter Biden had served. I used my own notes from the call to hand-correct the transcript.

And yet, though Tim Morrison had agreed with my changes, my corrections on those two points would never make it into the final version. At that point, I had no idea, of course, that the transcript would one day be made public, but I can say now that the version that was released was not fully accurate.

A few days after my first meeting with Eisenberg, he spoke to me again. This time, he warned me not to tell anyone else about what the president had said on the call. This seemed strange, too. Such coordination was natural and necessary. I was point person for the ongoing, all-day-every-day, full-speed interagency effort to get Ukraine policy back on track. Now I had new and important information on what had pulled the policy so widely off track: the president's domestic political scheming. Aside from Eisenberg, I'd read out portions of the call to only two people, both with full clearance and both included among those with a need to know, and while I had no intention of discussing the call more broadly, I wondered why he would ask me to limit coordination if there was nothing wrong with the call.

He soon added something else surprising. Clearly trying to suss out whether I'd communicated with anyone else, and what my own views on the call were at the moment, he said that somebody at CIA had also lodged a complaint with the Office of the Intelligence Community Inspector General regarding the July 25 call. His implication was that I was the source for the CIA reporter. I wasn't sure what to make of this, and I wondered if one of the two people I'd spoken to had made the complaint—but I also didn't dwell on the matter or have time to puzzle it out.

The July 25 phone call would turn out to be a watershed for the country, and for my own life, but that's not how I saw it at the time. I simply did my duty. My urgent professional effort, from well before July 25 and in the ensuing days and weeks, remained to pursue the many challenges facing my portfolio. Among so many other complicated matters, reversing the hold on the Ukraine funds was the foremost (and, at this point, nearly the only) thing on my mind.

Typically, the pace of government slows down in August, even at NSC, and especially in my area, because Europe itself traditionally shuts down. I therefore had a two-week break scheduled to begin August 3. But there was no expectation of a summer slowdown this year: we were still laser-focused on stabilizing the Ukraine situation before Russia took advantage of what would appear to be weakening U.S. commitment. The Sub-PCC that I'd formed for that purpose now became a Deputies Committee, so I was still putting in fourteen- and sixteen-hour days, organizing vast reservoirs of professional expertise, leading complicated meetings, and briefing high officials in government. Fighting through the effects of sleep deprivation had become a familiar feeling.

Also on my plate was an upcoming late-August/early-September trip, scheduled for NSA Bolton and key aides. For me, this was an especially exciting prospect, as the group would be visiting Ukraine, Moldova, and Belarus, the three European countries in my portfolio, with me accompanying NSA Bolton to each. The Belarus leg was especially critical. It would be the first time since 1994 that senior U.S. officials would meet with officials of the nation known as the "last dictatorship in Europe." Russia had been trying to cement Belarussian interests to its own aims, and it was our policy to counter that effort while persuading Belarussian leadership of the need for free and fair elections. My preparation for the trip required hours of detailed planning, thorough analysis, and a deep understanding and organizing of many layers of the officialdom of three very different governments.

Given everything that was going on, I asked Tim Morrison if I should really be taking my two-week leave on August 3—maybe

I should change my tickets, leaving the return open? But Tim was certain that I should go, not make any changes to my plans. So Rachel, Ellie, and I went to Breckenridge, Colorado, and then on to Mesa Verde, Colorado: the amazing cliff-dwelling site of the indigenous people of the Southwest. These rooms carved out of red stone are like ancient apartment buildings. We marveled at the beauty and deep sense of history that Mesa Verde affords, and I was proud to see Ellie climbing the rickety ladders alone. We also went rock climbing and ziplining. One day, we rented a kayak and took it out on pristine, frigid Dylan Lake, dipping our paddles in the perfect reflection of the big, clear Colorado sky. Though Rachel declined, Ellie and I took some bracing dips in the freezing water.

And that's when my work cell rang—while we were way out on Dylan Lake. I had to get back to Washington right away. We started paddling.

This wasn't really such a surprise. Tim was clearly unprepared to do all the planning for the three-legged Bolton trip without me, so I'd already mentally gamed out my possible exit from vacation. We drove all the way to Oklahoma, where Rachel and Ellie would stay for a visit with Rachel's ninety-three-year-old grandmother while I flew back to Washington alone.

On arrival, I found a situation at NSC that was growing increasingly strange. On August 12, an unnamed CIA whistleblower had filed a complaint against the president; clearly, this was the person Eisenberg had been referring to earlier when trying to find out if I'd been the source. The complaint was to be assessed for its credibility by the inspector general for the intelligence community, Michael Atkinson, before being forwarded to the chairs of the House and Senate Intelligence Committees. It detailed a scheme by the president to use "the power of his office to solicit interference from a foreign country in the 2020 U.S. election," and it named Giuliani and Attorney General Bill Barr as central figures. The whistleblower, evidently a member of the intelligence community, said that while he or she was not directly a witness to most of the events described, multiple reports from sources were mutually corroborating. The first major item in the complaint was the July 25 phone call between President Trump and President Zelensky.

I wouldn't be privy to the actual complaint until the rest of the country was, on September 13. When I did read it, the description of the call sounded intimately familiar to me. Still later, I would testify that I didn't know who the whistleblower was—truthfully, as the whistleblower's identity remains a matter of speculation. I can't know whether one of the two people to whom I reported the president's wrongdoing was the person who filed the complaint. The whistleblower complaint says that multiple officials reported the substance of the call, so I could be their source, but I can't say definitively. I did know, however, that Tim Morrison would likely conclude that I was the whistleblower's sole source, as would John Eisenberg. The impropriety of Eisenberg's decision to hide the call transcript on the secret server was a feature of the whistleblower's complaint.

And yet—and this may seem strange in retrospect—I was by no means living in anticipation of some retaliation against me personally for having reported through the proper channels what the president said on that call. I'd reported what I knew and then gotten back to work. I believed there was a process. I believed that the process would work to rectify the situation.

Given that I'd been called away from a family vacation so urgently, I found my workload those first couple of days back a bit light. The upcoming Bolton trip, so exciting to me, was complicated and delicate, however, and over the next weeks, I worked closely with Tim Morrison. I was even beginning to think our relationship was improving, that Tim and I were learning to work together. There still seemed to be potential for our shared goal: improving the Ukraine situation. And I was still absorbed in putting together a presidential decision memo to lift the hold on security funds. The president was scheduled to meet with President Andrzej Duda, in Poland, on the eightieth anniversary of the outbreak of World War II; President Zelensky would be attending as well, and the event was to include the signing of a new agreement on energy cooperation between Poland, Ukraine, and the United States. As it would dovetail with the Bolton trip to eastern Europe, we figured some repair work on Ukraine could be carried out at the Poland meeting.

To prepare the president for his meeting with the president of Poland, Tim gave me a new task. Instead of the usual talking points—we now knew the president could easily stray from such prep work and make statements contrary to policy—I had to write up highly simplified cards, each with a single point. This was basically a dumbed-down cheat sheet.

But then President Trump bailed on the Poland trip, and my work on the cheat sheet was abruptly interrupted. While he claimed a need to stay at home to cope with oncoming Hurricane Dorian, many of us suspected that he didn't want to meet Zelensky. It was decided that Vice President Pence would make the trip instead, and my cheat sheet work migrated to Jennifer Williams, the vice president's advisor on European and Russian affairs. It made sense to involve Jennifer, but it was unusual to leave me out. And I could get nothing specific from Tim regarding my role in the upcoming Bolton trip.

The absence of the normal.

I never saw it coming.

At the end of August, with the Bolton trip impending, Tim told me I wouldn't be going.

"Why?" I said, shocked.

The trip was in the region under my direct purview. It was the kind of trip on which I routinely would have been included—similar to my trip with Bolton to Geneva and Kyiv the year before. This trip's success even depended to some degree on my presence.

"It makes no sense," I protested.

"Because I said so" was more or less Tim's response. He was going without me, he said.

But Tim had no knowledge of the area. No other director had been excluded like this.

We began a tense email exchange. I told him that his answer wasn't good enough; I needed a reasonable explanation. He came up with a fake one: "Bolton's not traveling with directors anymore," he wrote.

I didn't push it further, but I was deeply disappointed—really, I was crushed, for a long moment.

The presence of the abnormal.

Soon I began to feel the effects of something I'd barely been registering. My officemate, Joe Wang, the other director for Russia, was working to undermine me. There was no love lost between Joe and me: after Fiona left, he had gravitated quickly to Tim Morrison. He and I shared a small office and had exchanged maybe ten words over the past three months, a significant deterioration in our relationship. Now I learned that Joe had launched a whisper campaign describing me as an inveterate leaker with poor judgment. (The House Republicans would later bring up these mischaracterizations of me, even trying to rope Fiona Hill's judgment into the charges, contrary to everything Fiona had ever said about me.) I didn't think he'd have shown that kind of malevolent initiative on his own: Joe had become very much Tim's guy.

My exclusion from the trip, and now this baseless whisper campaign—I was starting to get the idea. Certain people within the National Security Council itself had become aware of, and were unhappy about, my reporting the presidential wrongdoing. Clearly those people included the very officials immediately responsible for managing such reporting: Tim Morrison and John Eisenberg. I had no direct indication of this, but it's possible that Ambassador Bolton, too, was unhappy with my decision to say what I knew—despite his open objections to Sondland's, Mulvaney's, and Giuliani's shenanigans, which he'd referred to with open disdain as a "drug deal." In any event, I could see that I was being sidelined and torn down.

In response to this dawning perception, I decided to handle the issue in my usual way: I would go at the problem directly to clear the air. I went to Tim Morrison and raised the issue of the July 25 phone call and my reporting of it to Eisenberg and asked Tim point-blank if I was being subjected to retaliation. Tim denied everything. He hadn't even known, he claimed, that I'd reported the call to anyone.

This didn't seem likely, even at the time. Later, under oath, Tim would swear that, throughout this whole period, he'd never known about my reporting on the call. That's certainly not true, given that

I explicitly raised the issue with him in my effort to clear the air. Tim didn't tell Congress the truth, and I don't think he told me the truth when denying retaliating against me.

Meanwhile, Tim went on the three-nation trip in my place, meeting with leaders in all the European countries in my brief—and the effects of sidelining a professional for political reasons became immediately obvious. Because Tim had no knowledge of the countries he was visiting, or of the officials with whom he was talking, he began constantly pinging my cell with quotidian questions. Having bounced back from my disappointment over the trip, I did my best to make myself useful from Washington. Tim also needed quick language translations and other basic information, which, as Rachel said (highly annoyed on my behalf), she would have known the answers to, and if she didn't, she could have googled them. Tim missed diplomatic opportunities on that trip, thanks both to his lack of involvement in the region and to his sidelining me.

In Poland, both NSA Bolton and Vice President Pence met with President Zelensky. At least those meetings, I thought, might get the hold on aid reversed. But no—we'd come to the end of that line. Any control I'd imagined the policy community exercising over the situation now went up in smoke.

Meanwhile, everything back at the White House started changing fast. Inspector General Atkinson deemed the whistleblower complaint credible and urgent. He forwarded it to the acting director of national intelligence, Joseph Maguire, reminding him that, by federal law, he had seven days to forward the complaint to the relevant committee chairs in Congress. At almost the same moment, the hold on the aid to Ukraine was reported in the press for the first time. And when Acting Director Maguire failed to forward the complaint to Congress within the legally required period, the inspector general notified Congress himself. That same day, three House committees announced investigations into the question of whether President Trump and Rudolph Giuliani had abused the foreign policy process to pressure Ukraine into actions intended to benefit President Trump politically.

The thing I hadn't predicted was actually happening: the president's whole Ukraine scheme—with its flashpoint, the wrongdoing that I'd reported—was going public.

And so, it turned out, was I.

CHAPTER 10

———

BIGGER THAN LIFE

———

On Thursday, October 17, I experienced the high point of my military career up to that moment when Maj. Gen. Bradley Gericke called to tell me that I'd been selected for Senior Service College. Many civilians may not know the honor involved in being selected for the U.S. Army War College. Offered to a small group of senior military and civilian leaders, War College attendance prepares the highest-achieving members of the officer class for service at the most sophisticated strategic levels of the national security community. My selection also meant I would be promoted to full colonel. This was far beyond anything I could have expected at the outset of my military service. Yet now I suspected that I might never get to attend War College. I might never get my promotion at all.

The evening before, I'd received a formal request from the U.S. House of Representatives to appear as a witness in hearings conducted by House committees looking into impeaching President Donald Trump. Risking ending the career that had brought me all the way to selection to War College and promotion to colonel, I was going to testify against my commander in chief.

I'd always had a visceral feeling that the president's phone call with Zelensky would be the impeachable issue. Like everybody else following the news, I knew the specter of impeachment had loomed over some of the president's other offenses. But it seemed to me that subverting the foreign policy of the United States and making it subject to a low deal to smear a domestic political opponent was a far graver offense than anything for which any other president had been impeached. For some time, though, I didn't think the issue would get to the point of impeachment. Obsessively focused on getting Ukraine policy back on track, I'd been hoping the president could somehow be reined in and walk back his improper quid pro quo.

But once the inspector general verified the whistleblower complaint as credible, that ship had sailed. The issue was going public, and "going public," I knew, meant impeachment. As the person who had reported the call up the chain of command, I would be on that ship, too, headed I knew not where.

I wasn't even sure impeachment was the right course of action. But that wasn't my call: it was up to the elected and accountable people in the legislative branch. All I could do was continue to report the facts so that the calls could be made by the civilian officials. I fully believed that at least some Republicans in Congress would see the president's behavior the way I did—as an obvious and unacceptable abuse of presidential power. Even if they didn't vote to impeach, or vote for his removal from office, the Republicans might vote to censure him. In retrospect, it's clear that I had a lot to learn about the workings of partisanship in this period in our history.

Fiona Hill had suggested earlier that I lacked a certain political acumen, that I was inveterately naïve—and my hopeful expectations of the Republicans in Congress may confirm her assessment, but even now I'm not so sure. At many times in our history, matters of grave national concern have overcome sheer, self-interested partisanship of the kind I was soon to confront on the part of Republican lawmakers in Congress. There had to be a path, I believed, for regaining American leaders' historic commitment to country over party. If we worked toward a better future together, hopefulness wouldn't necessarily have to equate with naïveté.

Then again, by the time I was called to testify, my optimism had already taken some hits. I'd been feeling the effects of retaliation by my colleagues and superiors since August, and further retaliation came in early September. Having been left off the eastern Europe trip critical to my brief, now I was excluded from the upcoming United Nations' General Assembly meeting in New York.

At first, this pattern of reprisal was more punishing to me than truly disabling. Some trips are, to a certain degree, vanity projects, and anyway, I continued to coordinate policy for my region: nobody else had the ability, so my bosses still depended on me to do my job. Yet it was becoming clear that they'd begun to see me as a political obstacle to the smooth progress of their own careers.

And the boss situation was changing. In early September, President Trump raised the idea of inviting the leadership of the Taliban to Camp David—right around 9/11—to discuss ending the long conflict in Afghanistan. NSA Bolton, arguing that we could draw down troops in Afghanistan without making a deal with terrorists, vehemently opposed this idea. The proposed talks were scrapped, but the president revealed his failed plan in a series of tweets, and on September 10, Bolton announced that he'd resigned his position as national security advisor. President Trump tweeted that he'd fired him, but in any event, Bolton was out at NSC, and Tim Morrison, the ultimate Bolton guy, had to know he'd soon be out, too.

But not yet. With Bolton gone, events started moving at head-spinning speed.

First, on September 11, the White House abruptly reversed the hold on funds to Ukraine. After all those months of ceaselessly trying, across the whole community of expertise, to persuade the president to act in accordance with U.S. interests and policy, we on the inside could see this miraculous reversal for just what it was: a transparent ploy to neutralize the investigation of the hold that the House had launched.

Then, for the same all-too-obvious reason, the president at last agreed to a bilateral meeting with President Zelensky. It was not to be the promised White House sit-down, but it was still a big opportunity. They scheduled it for September 25, during the meeting of the UN General Assembly from which I'd been excluded. The president was clearly scrambling, in his usual chaotic and grudging way, to make a show, and only a show, of getting Ukraine relations normalized enough to dull the scrutiny he was now drawing.

The White House even came up with a false rationale for having placed the initial hold on the funds. Instead of the real reason—

which of course was to smear Joe Biden through his son—the administration now claimed that there had been a major, ongoing presidential policy review of Ukraine and that this review had only now recommended continuing the aid. The administration pointed the press and the public toward my big interagency effort—it really was a major policy review—while falsely framing it as a top-down presidential effort. Our review was of course exactly the opposite: a bottom-up effort urging the president to reverse a hold he'd already made. There's usually a kernel of truth in the big lie. This one was clever.

As an NSC officer, I wasn't about to publicly deny the White House cover story. I just hoped to leverage it, to use that lemon to make lemonade, locking down the security funding for Ukraine—for we were suddenly busy in a new way. We had to spend the suddenly released money and get Ukraine back in shape as a buffer against Russian aggression in eastern Europe. The administration was claiming publicly that withholding the funds had caused no problem for Ukraine's security. That, too, was false. We had to work fast.

Then, less than a week after the hold was reversed, everything changed again. The whistleblower complaint became public. Now the cover story for the hold on funds was revealed as a lie, and the truth about the president's Ukraine scheme was all over the news. Both the American public and I could finally read the whistleblower complaint, and I saw right away that its narrative, so painstakingly written and documented, was sure to be credible to large segments of the public. I knew, of course, that what it said about the July 25 call was true in every detail.

When the whistleblower complaint came out, I finally understood more fully why I was being routinely pushed aside and excluded.

Tim Morrison and John Eisenberg already knew the story the complaint told. They'd known it since July. Tim himself had been on the call, and Eisenberg had heard the story directly from me, when I duly reported my concern to him; the complaint even named Eisenberg as the person who moved the call transcript onto the secret server.

Once the complaint went public, it got even harder for me to do my job. Now I wasn't just being excluded from trips to my region; I was being left off many important calls that I would normally have been on. In one case, the supposed reason was that I lacked access to the relevant classified information.

I did my usual thing and confronted Tim: why was this happening? And Tim did his usual thing and gave only noncommittal answers. His rationale for leaving me out of the General Assembly meeting in New York was the absurd idea that NSC directors weren't attending, though some of my colleagues did end up going.

I was fed up with these reprisals. I had some extra vacation time, and it was "use it or lose it." Rather than sit in the office and brood over my absence from a critical meeting at the United Nations, and already having plans to go to Rhode Island for my cousin's wedding, I took that week off.

So I was on vacation when, on September 24, House Speaker Nancy Pelosi announced that the House would begin an impeachment inquiry on the basis of the information revealed in the whistleblower complaint. "The President must be held accountable," Speaker Pelosi said. "No one is above the law."

The next day, when President Trump finally sat down with President Zelensky at the General Assembly, after all those months of our dedicated effort, I wasn't there. Instead, I was eating with Rachel and Ellie in a Five Guys. This was already a long way from where I'd been just a few months before. I knew my life was changing because of my commitment to doing what I thought was right. I just couldn't tell how much.

As the House impeachment committee started calling witnesses for closed-door testimony, I found myself going into a mode that was both totally new and strangely familiar. I was in unknown territory. There were dangers everywhere, but this time around, I didn't know exactly what those dangers might be.

And yet my gut responses were familiar to me. Navigation is everything. I'd been in unknown terrain before, facing dangers of unknown origin. And I'd long since gotten used to studying and digesting new information quickly and readying myself and others for decisive action. It had taken me too long to see that I was being attacked from within NSC that I'd only barely registered that I was bleeding. Now I knew what was happening, that I'd taken hits, but I was still standing and still in fighting shape.

I started studying the situation, developing a strategy and getting into position to continue to do the right thing in the right way. The House, I saw, was beginning its investigation by bringing in senior people, the bigger fish. I deduced that that's how these investigations worked. They weren't starting on the ground, with people like me, the lieutenant colonel who had been on the actual call—I looked like nuts and bolts. Early on, for example, they called Kurt Volker, the U.S. special representative for Ukraine negotiations, who resigned his position on September 27, only hours after being called as a witness; they also called Fiona Hill. Because the testimony was closed-door, it took days to be released, so there was a lag in considering its possible effects. Still, from watching the process and analyzing the situation, I began to figure out what it was I would have to do.

In that context, I assessed my preparedness for engagement and quickly concluded that I was not equipped for the coming challenges. I saw that all those big-fish witnesses had lawyers. Clearly, I too would need representation. But how was I going to pay for it? I recalled that sometime earlier, my officemate Joe Wang had advised me to buy professional liability insurance—the kind of insurance that can pay legal expenses in certain situations. Partly out of sheer stubbornness—I didn't like or respect Joe—I hadn't taken his advice. I'd been foolish.

One Thursday night, as Rachel and I were talking in bed before going to sleep, I mentioned the whistleblower report, and I told her for the first time that I'd been on the call.

"Maybe tomorrow see about professional liability insurance," I suggested. Then I rolled over and fell dead asleep.

Rachel says she stayed awake all night. She was already seeing where this was going. I didn't—not yet.

My strategy was to go step by step and try to make simple, correct decisions each time. I'd begun taking these measures of the terrain and arming myself appropriately because I was already planning to testify if called. I had no doubt about that. As with my decision to report the president's wrongdoing, the decision to testify wasn't one I struggled with—though there was, in fact, a conflict involved: the president was generally prohibiting members of the administration from testifying. Some key witnesses, like former NSA Bolton, declined to testify, and some resigned in order to do so; others had already left the administration.

But there had been no explicit instructions to me not to testify, and I didn't feel called upon to resign. The Office of Legal Counsel wasn't about to go so far as to try to prevent testimony legally. In the oath I'd taken many times as a military officer, there was a clear duty to the Constitution. If that oath were now in conflict with the general orders of my commander in chief, then this was a unique, maybe even unprecedented situation, brought on by President Trump's own efforts to subvert the Constitution. I wondered how many times in U.S. history an officer's obligations to the commander in chief conflicted with the oath to support and defend the Constitution of the United States. Probably never—yet here I was, facing this same conflict for a second time. I felt that any inherent conflict left the decision up to me, as a matter of conscience, and I was fully resolved to continue on the path I'd begun on July 25, when I walked into Eug's office straight out of the call and started taking actions that had now brought the country to crisis. I'd told the truth to the appropriate people then. I would tell the truth to the U.S. Congress now.

I knew that trouble lay ahead. Yet, as in combat, a state of calm was settling over me. You never know if the lessons you've learned will hold up under the most serious tests of character, courage, and morality. I'd never faced a test like this—a historic test not only of my own moral compass but, far more important, of the nation's soul and will. I'd been placed at the center of a crisis, and as I began navigating this vast new landscape of high-stakes governing, constitutional law, and wrongdoing, I felt confident that I'd learned what I needed in order to act as I should. I had to trust my gut.

My earliest teacher in the lessons I was now applying to this challenging new situation was, of course, my father. Along with my wife, he was the most influential person in my life. At eighty-seven years old, he remained the same fiercely determined man who had grown up in the Urals during the Nazi invasion, overcome vicious anti-Semitism to rise to the top of his profession in the Soviet Union, and arrived in the United States with almost nothing, only to reestablish himself here and give us the best possible opportunities as Americans.

At the end of September, Rachel and I were driving with my dad to my cousin's wedding in Rhode Island when conflict erupted between him and me. It was a family scene. I was at the wheel, with my dad riding shotgun. Rachel was in the second row next to my mom; my mom's cousin sat in the third row. While we traveled, Rachel was on her phone searching for the right lawyer. Having deduced that I could easily be viewed as the whistleblower's source, she'd seen right away that my testimony would be explosive.

My dad suddenly began arguing with me. I must, at all costs, he insisted, avoid testifying against the president. His anxiety blew up, and soon he was yelling. "Support the president!" my dad demanded. "Do whatever the president wants!"

My father had lived in this country for forty years, yet there was no doubt in his mind that, when push came to shove, the highest levels of the U.S. government were bound to resemble the Soviet system he'd fled—that even here, any challenge to authority, any divergence from quid pro quo and backroom corruption, would be met only by reprisal, character assassination, the end of a career, and maybe even worse. Despite his success in it, he'd abandoned the Soviet system, leaving everything behind, not for financial advantage but because America is supposed to be fundamentally different. But he didn't trust that difference to hold up in this crisis.

Still, I believed that my dad had to know, on some level, that America was different from the Soviet Union. My own career was living proof. From seemingly less-than-promising beginnings, I'd enjoyed a successful rise in the military and foreign policy establishments not because I'd learned to suck up, go along, play the system, cold-bloodedly gauge my own advantage, avoid risk, and refrain from expressing myself. Just the opposite: I'd enjoyed that success through a series of challenging encounters. I'd discovered a personal passion, taken calculated risks, spoken my mind, and trusted my gut. And I'd been encouraged and rewarded in that process by great mentors. My life story wasn't just any career success story or story of service to one's country. It was a particularly *American* story. When I came in conflict with corrupt authority, I acted on the values that had brought me so far. And it was from my dad himself that I began to absorb those values before I could even speak.

That was a tough car ride. At least as stubborn as I, my dad kept yelling. Rachel tried to block out all the drama and concentrate on finding us a lawyer. My dad would remain immovably certain, for some time to come, that I was being totally naïve about the workings of power. He saw me taking an uncalculated risk and acting on impulse—the kind of thing Eug and I had been notorious for as kids—and placing myself in a danger I didn't understand. But I wasn't about to self-deter now, no matter what my dad said.

Of course he was right, to a degree. I was already experiencing reprisals from a career-oriented, conflict-averse officialdom of just the kind my father had encountered in the Soviet Union. But I was also certain—immovably certain, and I remain so—that the behavior of people like Tim Morrison, John Eisenberg, and Joe Wang didn't tell anything like the whole story of government in the United States. I was certain, and I remain certain, that here, in the end, right matters.

My dad had another reason to oppose my decision. He believed I was wrong about what I'd heard the president say on the phone call with President Zelensky. He figured I must have missed something—that President Trump wouldn't do anything improper, much less criminal. Like many Russian émigrés in New York and around the country, my dad had become a die-hard Trump supporter. Despite all the prejudice he'd suffered as a Ukrainian Jew in the Soviet Union, despite his inspiring story as an American immigrant, despite his fleeing a system of corruption to reap the moral benefits of liberal democracy—despite all this, he'd bought into the antiliberal prejudice that pervades the Soviet émigré community here. Encouraged in part by well-organized propaganda coming out of Putin's Russia, there is a form of Russian American right-wing nationalism, one strangely allied with U.S. nativists, that casts the Democratic Party as a latter-day revival of the old, hated Soviet Communist Party. Among Russian and Ukrainian Jews in the United States, such tendencies are further bound up in suspicion of anything seen as less-than-fervent support for Israel. To my dad, the prospect of my giving aid to the Democratic majority in the House put me on the wrong side of history.

During that wedding weekend in Rhode Island, I began taking serious stock of what this developing situation would demand of me. I was going up against not only the president of the United States, whose poor character I'd seen up close, but also the father I loved and deeply respected and from whom I'd taken so much that formed my character.

But I was ready. I knew that even though my dad couldn't see why I was doing what I was doing, I was acting on the basis of what I'd learned from him. I was also confident that he would always side with me when it counted.

_____

Rachel had quickly gotten us some superb help and advice. Steve, a high school friend of her late father, was a highly connected Republican attorney in Washington, a classic K Street lobbyist with a background in the Reagan administration and clients like the National Rifle Association. Steve had a reputation as a killer lawyer. He also had a warm spot for friends, and for Rachel. And his close connections with the Trump White House really amounted to a direct line.

A super-connected Republican lawyer like Steve may have seemed, at first glance, like a counterintuitive choice, but I'd long since learned that once you've decided to take action, you must do it as strategically as possible. The basis for our strategy was to avoid tipping off the White House and its allies in Congress to the explosion I was going to set off with my testimony. To that end, Steve, smart and deeply experienced, advised me to get a GOP legal team. The reason: I was still under the radar. It wasn't clear to the legislators, or to many administration officials, that this lieutenant colonel with a name little known to the press and public was an eyewitness source for what had become a national crisis. Having GOP lawyers would add to this soothing effect on my opponents.

Tim Morrison went another way: having done what he could to stifle the truth I'd reported, he hired a liberal law firm, in the hope of ingratiating himself with the Democrats. I wasn't trying to ingratiate myself. I was trying to ensure my ability to take the action I wanted to take, to say what I knew without being blindsided. The key, therefore, was to seem innocuous and draw no undue attention. I understood Steve's approach. It was like being in a TOC, moving military forces carefully, quietly, into a tightening cordon while trying not to spook the target. We would give my opponents as little time as possible to make any preemptive moves against me.

Steve gave me another piece of lawyerly advice. Using highly technical terms, he told me to "shut the fuck up": I wasn't to take any public stands or speak to anyone but Rachel and my lawyers about what I was thinking. I was learning something new about professionalism. Here was Steve, the ultimate GOP insider, with strong feelings about taking care, especially, of Rachel and Ellie, giving us the full benefit of his long, deep expertise solely on our behalf as his clients.

For all my growing respect for legal professionalism, however, I was soon forced to push back against some of the advice my lawyers were giving me. Steve had gotten me to Michael Volkov, the brilliant Republican white-collar defense attorney who would represent me during the hearings. (When it came to finances, both lawyers agreed to reduce their fees to the limits of the personal liability insurance policy I'd bought. In any event, the insurance company rejected my claim, so both lawyers worked pro bono, a generosity for which I'll always be grateful.) But when I first met with Mike, on October 13, his overall assessment was a reassuring "You'll be fine." Despite his strategic acumen, Mike was reading me as a little fish, somebody unlikely to draw much scrutiny and more or less safe from harm. Even Steve, when advising me to hire a GOP legal team, believed he was only doing appropriate overkill. My lawyers, though superb, didn't see right away the potential impact of what I was going to reveal.

The army's attitude was similar. On October 16, when I took the call from Major General Gericke informing me of my selection for Senior Service College, I revealed to him that I'd just been called to appear—the first time I notified anyone in the army that I'd been on the now-infamous July 25 phone call. I knew that my life might be cleaving in two at that very moment: the crowning point in my military career set against my potentially career-ending testimony against a sitting president.

But the major general didn't have much of a reaction to what I told him. From a standard army point of view, I was just a lieutenant colonel. It seemed unlikely I would have anything significant to do with the big political picture of a presidential impeachment.

If I'd hoped to come in under the radar, I certainly was succeeding.

At work, things were strange as well. There was new and confused leadership at NSC. On September 18, Robert C. O'Brien—in a normal administration, a third- or fourth-tier type—was appointed to replace John Bolton as national security advisor. A lawyer with no deep expertise in national security, O'Brien had recently made news when, as the president's appointee on international hostage negotiations, he'd attended the assault trial in Stockholm of Rakim Athelaston Mayers, the American rapper known as A$AP Rocky, and pressured the Swedish government to release the defendant. That effort had come at the behest of reality TV star Kim Kardashian West, who had asked Jared Kushner, the president's son-in-law, to seek the president's help in the case. Now Robert O'Brien was national security advisor for the United States.

As expected, my immediate boss, Tim Morrison, the Bolton acolyte, was fired early in October. He was replaced by Andrew Peek, who would stay only three months. Meanwhile, a policy reformulation for the agency was ongoing. The White House had told O'Brien to whittle down the size of NSC. Everybody there was just trying to figure out what all these changes might mean.

Meanwhile, I carved out two weekends for preparing my closed-door testimony. The lawyers and I spent many hours on the preparation, which proved a challenging new process for me—draining, like the hyperrealistic trainings I'd preferred as an officer, pushing the men well beyond what they thought they were capable of. The prep sessions were deliberately tiring, with no break, and they exhausted me.

Even setting up the sessions was demanding: we were mindful of potential surveillance, so we used encryption to communicate. We'd meet at Steve's town house near the Capitol building and at a short-term rented office space in town, where we'd repeatedly review the whole story and where I was then subjected to rigorous mock questioning.

As I responded to the practice questions, the lawyers' advice, not surprisingly, was to avoid characterizing people and situations in my answers and to volunteer little information. That was good advice, and I learned it fast. But they had a related tendency—especially our family protector, Steve—to coach me to give nonanswers, to deflect. The idea was to stymie hostile questioners and run out the clock. It was a standard way to go. Some of the impeachment witnesses—Gordon Sondland is a good example—were doing this, calculating their statements to minimize career and reputational risks, results that lawyers naturally want for their clients.

For better or for worse, though, that wasn't what I intended. I was learning from my lawyers, but they would also have to learn from me: I had my own approach to calculated risk. I had a specific, on-the-ground goal, a truth I intended to tell. Also, I was still infantry, dedicated to always being forward—though, of course, always in a strategic way. It was simply an unavoidable fact that I planned to volunteer a good bit of information. Some dissonance thus developed between my instincts as a military officer and my lawyers' instincts for minimizing client exposure at all costs.

At first, for example, they wanted me to memorize and repeat fully scripted answers to all likely questions. This went against every one of the hard-won abilities in which, by now, I had confidence. I come from the mission command philosophy—military officers know a mission's intent and get guidance on fulfilling it, yet they are expected to draw on everything they've learned to improvise creatively in conditions that are bound to be shifting and complicated. In a hostile environment, you have to be ready to respond flexibly, even while keeping overall goals and doctrines in mind. This approach applies everywhere. In my National Security class at Harvard, I learned how to do a deep dive on a topic, navigating volumes of material to put out a quick position paper. I'd applied that knowledge when leading interagency efforts at NSC, too. You get a good feel for the landscape, talk to the top people, weigh the best guidance and advice—and only then do you operate freely in pursuit of your goals. You don't memorize and parrot sources or advice; you draw on them as needed. That's what I wanted to do under questioning by Congress.

In the legal prep sessions, I also found myself drawing on my old military training, including what I'd learned about resisting adversaries' interrogation techniques. For each choice before me, I would make the simplest assessment and act on the basis of right and wrong, never overthinking it or attempting to strategize the way I would for my day job. The stakes were too high, and the situation too complex, for me to take any other approach. My only strategy was to tell the truth. That's the easiest path, because you don't have to keep your story straight. Our nation's elected officials are required to make the big decisions; my role, my *obligation*, was to provide them with the factual testimony on which such decisions would be based. I felt pretty sure that all my impulses would enable me to navigate an experience that would be like none I'd ever encountered.

Like many of my best superior officers, my attorney Mike Volkov ended up acquiescing in my plan to take my own approach. We dispensed with the rote, nonanswer approach and developed a way to answer where each question was turned to account and each answer told part of a larger story: the truth I wanted to impart. This required me to think on my feet, but thinking on my feet is a lot more natural to me than trying to commit answers to memory and living in fear of slipping up.

I was set to testify on Tuesday, October 29, and had to prepare an opening statement. Reviewing all the previous witness depositions that had been made public, I saw that while each had made a persuasive, professional case for their views on foreign policy, they hadn't attempted to connect on a more personal basis with the ordinary Americans who were following the impeachment hearings on TV. As I had a personal story to tell, I decided to begin my statement with my career of service and my immigrant family's American Dream. I thought if I provided that context, there was a chance that a lot of Americans would understand why I had to do what I was doing.

Talk about personal: Rachel's brains, sensitivity, and facility with clear thinking and writing were invaluable to my shaping the opening statement. She and I wrote it together, with some creative input from a couple of her friends—we called it the Suburban Moms Writers' Guild. Because we had workers in the house carrying out a major kitchen renovation, Rachel and I huddled upstairs in Ellie's room on Monday, the day before my testimony, to go through the final draft word by word; then I sent it to my legal team for their final approval. When Ellie got home from school that day, I helped her do her makeup for her Halloween costume; then we went to a Girl Scout Halloween party. During the event, I called my legal team one more time. Everything looked good. They then sent my opening statement to the House Permanent Select Committee on Intelligence.

Rachel still remembers the drive home from that Halloween party. We chatted about the logistics of getting me into DC the next morning for the testimony. We picked up my dress uniform from the dry cleaner. Looking back, we can see that those were our last couple of hours of normalcy. Today, in our life as a family, there's Before Impeachment and After Impeachment. We didn't know that afternoon that we were still living Before Impeachment.

The lawyers had, meanwhile, leaked my opening statement to the *New York Times*. (Now that we'd sent it to Congress, we had plausible deniability: the leak might have come from someone in the House.) This, too, was part of the strategy. Giving my opening statement to the press on the eve of my testimony was a preemptive move intended to help us take control of the public narrative. Everything I was going to say had been very tightly held, so far, in part to protect my promotion to colonel and my selection for War College, and it had been easy to stay low-profile: I was obscure, and I'd made no public attack on the president. We'd given no one any reason to suspect that I was about to describe, as an eyewitness, the entire scheme that the president's people had cooked up for subverting Ukraine policy; to confirm the whistleblower's account of the quid pro quo on the July 25 call; and to reveal that, back in July, I'd immediately reported what I knew up the chain of command.

Rachel and I therefore expected my statement to come as a bit of a bombshell for the House Republicans, putting them on the back foot and giving me an edge when starting my testimony. What we didn't expect was that it would come as a bombshell for all of America. Once we got home from the Halloween party, Ellie went upstairs to get ready for bed, and Rachel and I began to put all the pins and decorations back on my clean uniform, ready for the next day's appearance. Putting them all in the right place takes some thought and care, so Rachel kept photos of my completed uniform on her phone for reference. When she went to look at those shots, she was startled to see she'd missed a huge number of calls and texts.

I grabbed my phone. It was the same.

Evidently, cable news was all over my opening statement—everybody from Fox News to MSNBC. "Who is Alexander Vindman?" The press was scrambling to find out, and to play it up.

First things first: we finished with my uniform and put Ellie to bed. Then we turned on the news. We didn't watch cable news regularly. We didn't even know how to find the channels. When we did find them that evening, what we saw was surreal—it might be a cliché, but *surreal* is the only word that fits. Every channel was reading my opening statement. They were talking about my family's immigration story and my military service, and it hadn't taken them long to pick up on the fact that I was going to be the first witness who had actually heard the now-infamous July 25 call.

When we turned on Fox News, Laura Ingraham's guests were John Yoo, the former Justice Department official in the George W. Bush administration, and Alan Dershowitz, the celebrity lawyer. They accused me of being a traitor to the United States.

Now we knew we were in a before-and-after moment. Hearing me called a traitor on a TV show viewed by millions sent our family into After Impeachment. Here was yet another new terrain. I now realized that I wasn't fully prepared for what I was about to face.

The next morning, as Rachel drove me into DC, I read the many texts, emails, and social media messages I'd received during the night, and we listened as CNN and NPR discussed my opening statement. Part of Rachel's and my shock at the big, sudden public reaction came from the fact that the press and the public were latching on to things that military families take somewhat for granted. I have a Purple Heart. So do many people whom Rachel and I know. I hadn't realized how resonant one's sacrifice on behalf of the country can be for so many Americans. The public sentiment in this regard was heartwarming, and I was to learn much more about it in the months to come.

I'd also never fully realized how disruptive, how circus-like and relentless, even how vicious and demeaning, media attention can be, thanks to the deliberately polarizing, reality-TV political culture that our country suffers from today. A switch had been flipped. A flood of attention had been unexpectedly unleashed. There was no turning back that tide. Rachel dropped me off at my attorney's hotel and went to spend the day with friends.

Soon, I was seated at the massive witness conference table in a secure room. I looked around the table, where the committee members sat. As I began my closed-door testimony, I knew that thanks to the big, crude narratives that drive a lot of our public debate, I'd been transformed overnight into a larger-than-life character— American hero? American villain?—in one of the most divisive political dramas in American history.

CHAPTER 11

TESTIFYING

I testified twice. First came the closed-door impeachment investigation on October 29, and then, in November, my testimony in the live televised hearing. Both times, I was the only military officer called.

When I gave my closed-door testimony, I was also the first witness who had been White House staff and the first who had listened in on the July 25 call. I wore my dress uniform, with all the pins in place, a decision that, I later learned, caused some public comment. In my day-to-day work at NSC, I wore business attire. For a formal appearance at the Capitol, however, the required attire was my ceremonial uniform. Each ribbon, tab, and badge has a specific story of importance to me. The rifle with the wreath over my left breast pocket and the strawberry lightning insignia on my right breast pocket attest to my combat service. The Overseas Service Ribbon with the numeral five attests to my five overseas tours, on many of which I dragged my family from one posting to another. The Meritorious Service Medals attest to my exceptional service at the Pentagon, in Moscow as an attaché, and as a Stryker company commander. The Purple Heart signifies my wounds in combat, the shrapnel I carry to this day. While the people taking in the whole uniform wouldn't know these stories, the overall effect attested to my commitment, credibility, and long career of service.

I felt fully prepared on that morning of the closed-door testimony, confident in my strategy, but I was surprised by certain aspects of the process. Those who have seen public congressional testimony may be surprised to know how much more intense a closed-door session can be. Mine was a ten-and-a-half-hour day, the longest testimony up to that point, and committee members on both sides allowed themselves to get far more heated than they ever would on camera. At times they even engaged in shouted mutual attacks over what I was and was not permitted to say—especially regarding anything that might reveal the identity of the whistleblower.

It was disappointing how openly hostile the partisan atmosphere got. Even with all my strategizing, I'd come into the closed-door session harboring some idealistic misconceptions. As an active-duty army officer, I'd hoped I would receive fairly evenhanded treatment from elected officials. Early on, however, I realized that the Republican members were unified in one goal: to defend the president at all costs. Truth was their enemy, so my conveying the truth made me their enemy, too. They weren't there, I realized, to hear and weigh testimony. They didn't see themselves as legislators performing the duties incumbent upon them under the Constitution. Instead, it was a purely adversarial procedure. The Republican members seemed to have rationalized taking a role as defense attorneys, going to bat for the president, fulfilling an attorney's duty to provide a client with the best possible defense, regardless of his guilt. Along with being a perversion of their constitutional duty, this was a tall order. Sometimes defense attorneys have to defend clients they know are guilty, and that's how the Republican committee members struck me that day. Later, I would wonder how many of those Republican representatives would regret that they'd served as enablers to the president, thus advancing many of the tragedies the United States suffered in 2020 and 2021.

They did their best to defend their client, but there wasn't much they could do.

Because I was insistent on telling what I knew while remaining relentlessly professional, I felt on firm ground. Faced with these hostile, hyperpartisan efforts by the Republicans, however, I did find myself drawing on my most elemental combat training: survive, evade, resist, escape (SERE). I decided to oppose the Republicans' attacks not by defending myself directly but by using my responses as a kind of master class in one of my areas of expertise: Ukraine as a key U.S. partner. By giving the larger context, I diverted conflict away from myself personally—a man cast by the Republicans as some supposed enemy of the president—and placed the dangers posed by the president's behavior in the larger national security picture. The strategy seemed to be paying off.

Then came the most challenging questioning: from Rep. John Ratcliffe, a Republican from Texas and a former prosecutor. Some had implied that in reporting what I'd heard on the July 25 call, I'd been out of line—that I'd countermanded the president's orders, violating the chain of command. This accusation generally didn't shake me. Chain of command is critical, as all military people know, and the idea of being lectured on it by congressmen who had never served struck me as preposterous. But as anyone who has served would know, not following an unlawful order is also a requirement of all who serve. And I'd reported everything to the appropriate people, with all the appropriate clearances and need to know. I was well within all correct procedures.

Representative Ratcliffe, however, was an adroit adversary. As he questioned me, at first I had trouble seeing where he was going. He was working the chain-of-command theme, but with a deeper nuance that I didn't fully catch.

Now my adrenaline was up. I sensed risk. I slowed down and became very careful.

His underlying effort, I began to see, was to lead me down a path where I would end up implicating myself for having bucked the president on behalf of my own policy goals regarding Ukraine— suggesting that it was I, and not the president, who was subverting U.S. policy in the region. If I wasn't careful, I might allow a false picture to emerge, one in which I'd be seen as running my own rogue Ukraine policy in direct opposition to what I'd heard the president of the United States say on the July 25 call. I had, for example, personally warned Ukrainian officials, including President Zelensky, against getting involved in U.S. domestic affairs. As Representative Ratcliffe and I went back and forth, I saw the trap he was trying to set.

In fact, I'd had those conversations with Ukrainian officials well before the July 25 call. And when I had them, I wasn't speaking on behalf of some policy of my own; I was relaying official U.S. policy, as arrived at by the whole interagency community of interest on

Ukraine and in full alignment with the messaging of John Bolton as the president's national security advisor. Even after the July 25 call, my bosses Tim Morrison and John Bolton had expressly told me that the president's quid pro quo deal did not in any way reflect a change in U.S. policy.

So as I began to understand the agenda behind Representative Ratcliffe's questioning, I did my best to make that case to him. Still, I'd say that he and I fought to a draw. Mike Volkov stepped in. I also resorted to running the clock a bit by offering valuable info on Ukraine. Of my adversaries that day, Ratcliffe was the one I admired. Though I disliked his implications, which were false, my admiration reminded me of my respect for our Russian counterparts. They're good at what they do. You have to think hard and work hard to oppose them.

I also appreciated the effort of the Republicans' chief counsel, Steve Castor. He had a job to do—cast as many aspersions on my testimony as possible—but he seemed to know that not many aspersions could realistically be cast. He did what he had to do, as a professional, without any undue hostility. Most of all, I admired Committee Chairman Adam Schiff and many Democratic representatives for living up to their oaths and conducting a fair inquiry, and the lead counsel for the Democrats, Daniel Goldman, for his smarts and competence.

During breaks, I got feedback from my attorneys, who were quite happy—though, of course, they mixed "It's going great!" with "Say less!" I was adrenalized, feeling pretty good. I almost wanted to ask Mike to pass on to Ratcliffe that he'd done an awesome job. I restrained myself, though.

When the Democrats were questioning me, I could relax a bit. They weren't coming after me. Both sides did a fair amount of speechmaking for the record, giving me time to think, with a sense of awe, *This is so much bigger than me.*

Although it was a long and challenging day, when I look back, I see that the questioning itself wasn't so difficult. It was when I emerged from testifying that I found myself in a whirlwind I'd been oblivious to all day.

My opening statement had been all over the news the evening before, of course, and I'd already been trying to get my bearings in that harsh spotlight. But the testimony that day was supposed to have been closed. This hadn't stopped members of the House, on both sides, from coming out and giving TV interviews during my testimony to frame it politically. This drove the never-ending cable and online political news all day. By the time I came out—drained and feeling like I'd been in combat—the warring sides had been obsessively narrating my role, and they weren't about to stop now.

This made me doubly glad that my statement was out there, presenting me in my own words. Twitter was now aflame. John Yoo was back on with the Fox News anchor Laura Ingraham to suggest that I was engaging in espionage for Ukraine. They mentioned my Ukrainian birth and my facility with languages to imply, scurrilously, some secret background to my career as a U.S. military officer.

If I'd been disappointed in the adversarial nature of the Republican legislators' approach, these media attacks were even more shocking. A lot of it was nasty, but Yoo's and Ingraham's suggestions that I had a dual allegiance were especially nefarious. For someone like me, that's an enduring smear. Fulfilling the role of foreign area officer requires high-level clearance. Things like what Yoo and Ingraham were saying, however baseless and venally motivated, can make you vulnerable to your opposite numbers in adversary nations, hampering your ability to operate. Clearly, they were trying to hit me where I lived.

Still, I got encouraging responses that surprised and gratified me. That evening, when Rachel and I went back to Mike Volkov's hotel to have a drink at the bar, I was startled when some guys there insisted on buying me drinks. Then another guy did. I was only beginning to gather that I was becoming a public figure—a recognizable one. The scurrilous negativity from some of the press was balanced out by the respect and positivity of the public.

Yet full-scale campaigns against me had now begun, originating mainly on Twitter. The weirdest one, exciting to Trump supporters and even to President Trump himself, came from a retired army lieutenant colonel, Jim Hickman, who, within days of my closed-door session, began attacking me on Twitter. He claimed to know me, and he branded me an "Obama globalist." A fringe-y, ranting follower of the QAnon mega-conspiracy theory, Hickman claimed that during a military exercise in Germany in 2013, he'd heard me bashing the United States to Russian officers—in Russian, supposedly, though Hickman doesn't speak the language—and because he was supposedly my superior officer at the time, he'd reprimanded me for it, he said.

If I remembered Hickman correctly, he was an analog simulations guy doing game play for military exercises. I certainly never reported to him. His bizarre fabrication irritated me mainly because a fellow officer was stabbing me in the back, but thanks to the symbiotic relationship between the Trump White House and the crazy fringe, Hickman's delusion was picked up by the far-right media and then amplified, as such things are today, by the conservative media. I tried to stay cool, but it was hard.

Donald Trump Jr. seized on Hickman's strange claims and

attacked me on Twitter on that basis—although I took any attack from that quarter as a badge of honor. Then President Trump, when asked about my testimony by reporters, picked up on the Hickman delusions. "You'll be seeing very soon what comes out," the president predicted for me on the South Lawn of the White House. Both the public and I would later learn that the president had some other wild stories about me in mind.

Happily, these creepy attacks sparked a defense of my integrity from some of the most credible people in the military and government. My old boss General Dunford, former chairman of the Joint Chiefs of Staff, called me "a professional, competent, patriotic and loyal officer." Michael McFaul, former ambassador to Russia, took on the Hickman fantasy directly. McFaul said he'd interacted with me in front of Russian officers and that I had "never once said anything near what this 'retired Army officer' claims."

I was deeply grateful for these expressions of support. Still, thanks to having done my duty as I saw it, I seemed to be continuously emerging from one unknown terrain and into another even more treacherous. I saw that this engagement was by no means over, that it was only getting rougher. If I was going to get through this, I was going to have to keep drawing on everything I knew about tradecraft, focus, judgment, clarity, and strategy.

The morning after the closed-door testimony, I went back to work at NSC, put my head down, and continued to do my job. I was no longer sure how long I'd be doing it or what the effects of my testimony might be. Watching reports of the others who were testifying in closed-door sessions, I was already thinking ahead to the possibility of having to testify publicly.

Meanwhile, we were making very little progress on the all-important matter of the Ukraine relationship. President Trump's meeting with President Zelensky at the UN General Assembly, which the president had agreed to only to try to conceal what he'd actually been doing with Ukraine, hadn't gone well, and there was no positive follow-up. I was still running a lot of meetings, and we were looking at Belarus and Moldova, too.

The president had agreed to a bilateral meeting in Ukraine, but we couldn't get it reliably scheduled. There was talk of sending the secretary of state instead, but then the meeting was rescheduled for January.

Focusing on my job was my main intention, but I was now continuously subjected to press inquiries regarding the impeachment, which I passed on to the NSC press office. Meanwhile, the right-wing media, led by Fox News, was in a rage to demolish my reputation by any means necessary, and it's hard to make good judgments when you're the target of vicious and unfair attacks in front of millions of people.

Two weeks before my public testimony, I met with my legal team. David Pressman, former ambassador to the United Nations for President Obama and now a lawyer at Jenner and Block, had come on board to deal with the most negative aspects of the public narrative: the Fox News defamation and the White House's retaliation alike. I'm a fighter; that's always been my instinct. But amid this media circus, I found myself disabled. Sometimes you can't take up the fight yourself; you have to use the systems and the lawyers. Otherwise, things will only get worse.

This is a lesson I still do not like having learned. It was the first time since I snapped and started whaling on that school bully back in Brooklyn that I couldn't stand up for myself.

I had hoped the army would do something publicly on behalf of my reputation. But my main military defenders, like General Dunford, were retired, and while I received lots of private outreach from lower-level people, no active-duty, higher-up officers said anything publicly in my defense. Institutionally, the army's desire to remain apolitical is understandable. Still, part of the army value system is to take care of your soldiers, and I was a soldier being subjected to baseless attacks for doing his duty.

This traditional army reflex only invited more abuse of the military by President Trump. The army's staying silent in my case was only a prelude to its being used as a prop during the 2020 Black Lives Matter protests in DC, when Mark Milley, the chairman of the Joint Chiefs, was roped into walking, in uniform, across Lafayette Square with the president immediately following tear gas attacks on peaceful protesters. Chairman Milley would later publicly apologize for that.

Despite the army's apolitical stance, in early November 2019, I was called in by the army chief of staff, Gen. James McConville, to discuss the situation. I understood this highly atypical meeting to be an opportunity for General McConville to get eyes on me, assess my character, and warn me to do the right thing, in the right way. To aid me, the army put together a cell consisting of attorneys, public affairs officers, and a congressional liaison to help me navigate the public testimony. Major General Gericke was assigned as my handler. From now on, the only consistent engagement I would have with the army would be through him.

On November 19, I testified publicly in the impeachment hearings.

I was somewhat more ambivalent about deciding to testify publicly than I had been about the closed-door testimony. I'd already had a taste of what becoming a public figure could do to my life, and I knew that what I'd experienced so far would be nothing compared to the firehose of attention I'd get after being seen by millions on TV testifying against President Trump in an impeachment hearing.

And it wasn't my life alone: I knew my family's life, too, was about to change in unpredictable ways. The reprisals and attacks were bound to become more extreme. My job at NSC would be even more surely on the line.

Still, I had a duty to testify, over and against the president's prohibition. A subpoena from a coequal branch of government had been issued and delivered, and it aligned with my own sense of personal and professional duty. I would do what I always did: jump in, let things cycle, and see where I landed.

To that end, the lawyers and I revived our prep sessions, which were somewhat less exhausting this time. We knew more than we'd known before, had a better sense of where the attacks would come from and on what basis. I'd been watching others testify publicly. I saw that Ranking Member Devin Nunes, a Republican from California, was taking on a newly leading role for the Republicans, and I saw how he was treating witnesses whose testimony reflected poorly on the president. He would no doubt make unfair implications and mischaracterizations of me, and I would have to work on not showing anger and remaining staunchly professional at all times while never giving in.

I also knew that my former boss Tim Morrison had brought the Joe Wang whisper campaign against me into the closed-door hearing, describing me to Congress as unreliable, a constant leaker, and a known problem at NSC. The Republicans would be sure to bring up Tim's lies, so I went into the hearing with receipts: Fiona Hill's report card on me.

I've said that the closed-door hearing had a surprising intensity, thanks to the open mutual hostility of the members. And yet, for me as a witness, the public testimony, while less acrimonious on the part of the members, was pretty stunning. This time, millions were watching live. Clips would be played and replayed on TV and would exist for all time on the internet.

As I was seated, again in uniform, in the august setting of the borrowed assembly room of the House Ways and Means Committee, the centerpiece of the Longworth House Office Building, across Independence Avenue from the Capitol, and as dozens of journalists with cameras between the witness table and the dais crowded me, I was keenly aware of the import of the moment, and I made sure I took my time. I was a key witness in only the third presidential impeachment hearing ever held in the history of our country.

I had written a new opening statement for my public testimony, and this one wasn't leaked; I sprang it on the members that morning. It was Eug who came up with the idea of focusing my statement on our dad's concerns about my testifying—a stroke of genius from my quiet inner voice. Instead of ducking the conflict that I was in with my father, I got to do what I always want to do in response to a challenge: run straight at it and take it on. I needed to remind my dad, Congress, the whole country, and even myself that despite all the country's flaws, and even despite this president's rank corruption, the United States is elementally unlike the Soviet Union, unlike Putin's Russia, unlike so many other weak countries where corruption doesn't just exist but determines all of life. I had to reassure my dad—and all of us—that while I was facing challenges as a result of telling the truth, I would be all right in the end. Because this is the United States.

Once Rachel and I had written the statement, she hounded me to rehearse it, both with her and on my own. I did, but not nearly enough. I'm always better speaking off the cuff and thinking on my feet than delivering remarks in a rigidly prepared mode, but reading a written statement can't be off the cuff, of course. To begin my day of public testimony, I stumbled a bit and made some slips. I knew Rachel would blast me later. Still, it would become overwhelmingly clear that the statement's focus on my dad's concerns, and on my faith in our family's adopted country, resonated powerfully with a lot of my fellow citizens.

Eug was in the hearing room as well. He made sure not to sit directly behind me, so the cameras couldn't capture him scowling whenever I was attacked. All day he sat there, as stone-faced as possible, steadily taking notes. His plan was to coach me during breaks if needed and to bolster and buoy me at every opportunity. I assumed his responses to my testimony would be more critical than the lawyers'—from childhood, we've always been free with each other, each trusting the other enough to get pretty tough when it's called for. Yet during the breaks, he was kind and complimentary about how my testimony was going. Now I really knew I was doing okay.

During the questioning, in keeping with my opening statement, I shifted tack, taking a different approach from that of the closed-door hearing. This time, instead of educating the members about the importance of the U.S.-Ukraine relationship—Fiona Hill and George Kent, publicly testifying before I did, had done a fine job of that—I set out to neutralize the Republican members' criticisms and reach the public. I clarified chain of command. I explained the duties of a military officer. I played it straight and refused to make myself the center of the narrative, focusing instead on the high value to the United States of the professional expertise of the whole military and diplomatic community, a great public resource not to be dismissed.

There were a few occasions when the Republicans' attacks on my character and my job angered me. They tried to suggest—without even a hint of evidence, of course—that my whole career of military service had some hidden agenda. They tried to diminish my standing as the Russia and eastern Europe expert at NSC. They even questioned why I would wear my dress uniform to testify.

There was no real content to any of these insinuations: the idea was to throw vague shade over what I was reporting, in the hope of muddying the clear truth about the president's wrongdoing. It's no fun to have to sit and take such sleazy attacks, but I worked very hard on not allowing myself to be provoked into a thoughtless response.

At one point, however, Ranking Member Nunes forgot to address me by rank, and I corrected him instantly. I intended that correction as a pitcher's brushback. Having seen his tone with previous witnesses, I wanted him to know that I was alert, ready, and not to be pushed around. When Rep. Jim Jordan, Republican of Ohio, referred to Tim Morrison's preposterous characterization of me as a leaker and a known problem at NSC, and even went so far as to claim that Fiona Hill had shared those concerns, I pulled out Dr. Hill's report card and read a very small portion of it into the record, without belaboring the point. "'Alex is a top 1% military officer and the best Army officer I have worked with in my 15 years of government service,'" I read. "'He is brilliant, unflappable, and exercises excellent judgment'—I'm sorry—'was exemplary during numerous visits,' so forth and so on. I think you get the idea." I stopped there. And that pretty much did it.

Again, Steve Castor did his job on behalf of the Republicans, and in a more professional way than most of the Republican members. He brought up the time Oleksandr Danyliuk, the head of Ukraine's NSC, offered me a job as defense minister for Ukraine. I guess that was intended to hint at the dual-loyalty slur John Yoo and Laura Ingraham had alleged against me. But I'd duly reported that somewhat surprising offer to my superiors, and of course there was nothing there. They were grasping at straws, and Castor's mild questioning again indicated to me that he knew it.

It was in my exchange with Rep. Sean Patrick Maloney, Democrat of New York, that I was able to reinforce the main themes of my testimony before Congress and the country. Really, they're the themes of my whole life. In response to Representative Maloney, I described my gut reaction to hearing the president make his quid pro quo: at first, I couldn't believe I was hearing a U.S. president baldly undermine our democracy by demanding Ukraine fabricate an investigation into a political opponent. I told Representative Maloney that I'd reported what I'd heard because it was my duty. And at his request, I read aloud, again, the penultimate paragraph of my opening statement. This time, I did not stumble or slip.

Dad, my sitting here today, in the US Capitol talking to our elected officials is proof that you made the right decision forty years ago to leave the Soviet Union and come here to the United States of America in search of a better life for our family. Do not worry, I will be fine for telling the truth.

"He would worry," Representative Maloney said, "if you were putting yourself up against the President of the United States, is that right?"

"He deeply worried," I said, "because in his context, there was the ultimate risk."

"And why do you have confidence you can do that and tell your dad not to worry?"

This was the question I most wanted to answer. I knew how many of my fellow citizens would hear me.

"Congressman," I said, "because this is America. This is the country I've served and defended, that all my brothers have served. And here, right matters."

My public testimony was brief compared to the closed-door session. Eug and I left the hearing room and headed home, and the next day, we went to work together at NSC. As we came into the office, my colleagues cheered me. This was an amazing show of support from my professional counterparts, below the political level, and it was an incredible feeling.

There was a second wave and crescendo of attacks on me, of course, and this time it was a far bigger one. Jim Hickman doubled down on his paranoid conspiracy mongering, and it got widely picked up. Sen. Marsha Blackburn, Republican of Tennessee, launched a preposterous tirade against me as someone who had badmouthed the United States to the Russians, and the president himself retweeted this. The attacks by Representative Jordan that I'd shut down during the testimony got retailed around the right-wing media circus. Tim Morrison's public testimony came right after mine, on the same day, and Tim not only lied under oath about what he knew and when he knew it but also lied about me with impunity.

I was also experiencing hostility within the NSC office—not

from my counterparts but from higher-ups. I was barred from attending official functions in the West Wing. I was even told not to attend the accreditation of the new ambassadors coming from the countries in my file. And I was vilified in the pro-Israel Russian émigré community. People even contacted my dad, asking him to speak out against me.

By this time, my dad was having none of the pro-Trump propaganda and was defending me against all attacks. Characteristically, though, he hadn't undergone some gigantic political transformation: he remained, and remains, conservative, and his high regard for Trump fell more slowly than you might expect, given the administration's treatment of me. Nothing if not stubborn, my dad used his own, internal grading system for judging Trump's performance. From a level of support of 95–99 percent, the president began a slow but steady decline in his estimation, based not only on the reprisals against me but also upon his own closer, day-to-day attention to presidential politics, inspired by my experience. Soon, my dad began unplugging from Fox News and the Russian émigré press.

Still, it took time for the president to sink below 50 percent on my dad's scale, even amid all that was going on for our family. I suspect my dad's attitude ended up serving as a kind of rough predictor for Joe Biden's 2020 election victory, when down-ballot Republican candidates would do well overall despite a rejection of Trump. While his overall politics didn't change, by the time I left NSC, my dad had pretty much had it with the Trump presidency.

To protect my family—now receiving threats at the house—and to get the administration to stop harassing me, I considered moving us out of our home and onto base, for security purposes. This would have served as a public relations brushback, but we decided to give it a few more days to see if things calmed down. I did get the U.S. Army Criminal Investigation Division to increase our security, though.

Our greatest effort as a family, however, was to refuse to allow the maelstrom of crude political attacks on me to shake us up. I'm grateful that Ellie was only eight during this period. Her main experience of the whole affair was seeing Daddy on TV, and she loved it: she especially liked Stephen Colbert's and Trevor Noah's late-night monologues on the hearings. (She knows Noah's "Baby Spy" skit by heart.) Now it's different. She's older and more attuned and sensitive to our situation. She asks whether people like Daddy or Trump.

But for all the virulent public negativity from the right wing, and from the Trump administration and its supporters, this was nothing compared to the outpouring of support from ordinary Americans who had seen or read about my public testimony. There were friendly pieces in the press, of course, but what most astonished me were the letters—yes, old-fashioned letters, sent by the U.S. Postal Service—the emails, the Facebook posts, the old friends who suddenly got in touch, the strangers who came up to me on the street, all expressing admiration for my testimony and pride in me as a fellow citizen. Our synagogue alone received thousands of pieces of mail to be forwarded to me, expressing love and support, along with thousands of dollars in donations contributed in my name.

I read every single piece of the mail I received. Exactly six constituted hate mail. In April 2020, when I started writing this book, the flood of support was still coming in. It's been a huge groundswell, a beautiful thing that has lifted me up by confirming what I said in my testimony. All the ugly noise of the attacks on me was drowned out by the loving embrace of the American public.

———

I'd said "Here, right matters," and a lot of people were picking up the phrase and using it. But right didn't matter at all, of course, to the administration.

A big retaliation was drawing near. And this time, I could see it coming from a mile away.

In January 2020, my parents came to our house for New Year's Eve. The Senate impeachment trial was happening, and there was little suspense surrounding what Senate Republicans would do. I knew that my days at NSC were dwindling. Once the trial was over and the president was acquitted, I could expect to be fired for my testimony. In the hope of leaving my whole portfolio in decent shape, I was doubling down at work, spending long hours on developing an action plan for promoting the bilateral relationship with Ukraine and the other countries in my purview.

On February 5, the Republican majority in the Senate voted to acquit the president of charges of abuse of power and obstruction of Congress. On the latter charge, the Republicans voted as one. On the charge of abuse, which reflected the behavior I'd begun reporting on July 25, only Mitt Romney of Utah broke with the party and voted guilty.

President Trump immediately started ranting on Twitter: those who had testified against him were evil, corrupt, and crooked. His press secretary at the time, Stephanie Grisham, meanwhile, told reporters that anyone who had hurt the president should pay. Seeking an orderly turnover, I cleared my desk, organized my files, and briefed my likely successor. As expected, within forty-eight hours of his not-guilty verdict, President Trump fired both me and Eug.

On Friday, February 7, I was working on emails and the last-minute handoffs when the NSC director for resource management entered my office abruptly, accompanied by one security officer. She gave me the spiel: "Please step away from your computer, leadership has determined your services are no longer required. Pick up any personal effects. You will be escorted from the building."

I had no personal effects. There was nothing on my desk, nothing further to remove. The security officer who would be escorting me out was an acquaintance; I'd even been in his office earlier that day, to ask whether the NSC security team would be investigating the White House's leaking to Republican congressmen my memorandum reporting the Ukraine job offer made by Danyliuk. Because I knew my firing could come at any time, I'd closed that visit by saying, "Don't we have an appointment later today?" We'd both chuckled somewhat ruefully. Now here he was to do the job.

Having wrapped everything up in advance, I left my office empty-handed. It felt like a better look.

We walked down the hall and took the elevator to the lobby. I'd had some thrilling and very difficult times here. I'd worked with some stellar colleagues, contributing everything I had to help achieve stability in eastern Europe, in the face both of Russian aggression in the land of my ancestry and of the wayward approach to vital national policy taken by President Trump. I was satisfied to know that the action plans I'd created at NSC for Ukraine and my other portfolio countries would go into operation shortly after I left. That was my legacy on behalf of the national security of the United States.

Now I walked out of the Old Executive Office Building.

What was next for me? As I left the building that day, punished for doing my duty and telling the truth, I could not know the answer.

CHAPTER 12

PROMOTION

President Trump's forcing me out of the National Security Council and out of the White House ended my upward move in the government foreign policy and diplomatic track I'd been serving ever since my first posting as a foreign area officer in Moscow. Any chances of further service at NSC were doomed, upsetting all my career aspirations for contributing to U.S. security in increasingly important positions. I was headed toward an unforeseen and unpredictable future.

I was still an army officer, however, and on track for promotion to full colonel. I had also been specially honored by selection for the U.S. War College.

But I didn't attend War College. I wasn't promoted to colonel.

And I'm no longer an army officer. The totality of the change in my life, and my family's life, and the pace of that change have surpassed anything I could have foreseen. In early 2020, after I testified, I had to face the most difficult and painful decisions of my professional life. Coming to terms with those decisions would turn out to be among the hardest things I've ever done. I had to apply the lessons of a lifetime in a whole new way.

As early as November, but more seriously in February, when my exit from NSC was looking imminent, I began considering the realities of my future. The week before I left, I had some preliminary conversations with the staff of the secretary of the army, Ryan McCarthy, and with Major General Gericke, the two-star general assigned to manage me through the testimony.

I was an active-duty officer. The army had been my home since 1999, when I completed the course at Fort Benning and was assigned to the 506th in Korea. And as a foreign area officer assigned to NSC, I still regarded the army as my home.

So if I was out at NSC, what was my next army assignment? My longer-range expectation was to receive my promotion and attend War College, which was not scheduled to begin until July 2020. But what about in the meantime?

At first, things looked more or less okay. A policy job at the National Defense University, in Washington, came up in discussions. That seemed a good option for me. Plus, I had another opportunity, possibly even a replacement for Army War College. If I received a strong recommendation from a serious higher-up, I could attend Stanford University's Freeman Spogli Institute for International Studies. And I had something better than a strong recommendation: the director of that institute was Michael McFaul, the former ambassador to Russia who had spoken on my support after my testimony. He wrote a letter to the army chief of staff, Gen. James C. McConville, a peer-to-peer request, asking him to place me at his Stanford program.

But it turned out the army wanted me sequestered in an army institution, far from the public eye. They turned the Stanford request down flat. It was then that I began to pick up on a whole new issue. It was subtle at first, but quickly grew into a big, blatant, painful new obstacle.

In the eyes of the Trump White House and its supporters in Congress and in the media, I was an enemy, of course; I understood all that. But to the army, I began to see, I was more like a liability, a headache, and a bad one—and all the army wanted was relief from the pain. I realized then, as I do now, that my situation was an unusual one for the army to have to deal with. A lieutenant colonel, obscure outside the upper levels of his profession, had jumped into the public consciousness as a national political figure, and the army doesn't like its officers to be national political figures. My decisions to report and testify may have seemed so untoward that nobody in the army knew what I might do next. Uncertainty causes anxiety. It must have seemed to the army that I'd be more under control at Army War College than Stanford.

I could handle that. More distressing, though, was when all talk of my taking the policy job at the National Defense University suddenly evaporated from my discussions with General Gericke. He didn't say so explicitly, of course, but as the tenor of my conversations with him shifted, I began realizing that the army's real wish was to move me away from the capital and the Pentagon altogether—to get me completely out of foreign policy and national security, where the action was and where I'd painstakingly developed knowledge that had proved invaluable. The last place they wanted me now was in U.S. policy for the critical danger zone of Russia, Ukraine, and eastern Europe. My hard-won expertise would no longer play a role at all.

This was a shocking realization and hard to accept. I knew that as an army officer, I remained subject to the mantra "the needs of the army." It's not the needs of the soldier; the soldier doesn't get to choose. Evidently, the army's need now was to remove me from the scene. Only weeks before, I'd been running enormously significant cross-agency meetings for the entire U.S. policy, diplomatic, and security communities; writing complicated top-level documents; briefing officials at the highest reaches of government; providing presidential talking points for calls with foreign leaders; and moving mountains to get Ukraine policy under control and regain some stability. I'd become used to bringing everything I had to the intensity of that level of service. Coping with minute-by-minute challenges of historic, high-stakes national and global issues was the air I breathed.

I don't know if I showed it, but I recoiled from one of General Gericke's ideas for my next move: an assignment to the new National Museum of the United States Army, in Fort Belvoir, Virginia. The museum was not yet open, and no specific position was discussed. There would have been no overt punishment in such an assignment: it could have been seen as a comfortable offer, really. But while it wasn't manning a radar station in Alaska, the proposed assignment was the closest equivalent that would keep me in Washington. I'd be not just out of sight but buried, not contributing to the ongoing security of the United States as I had my entire career. Plus, I now had to put up with cracks from both Rachel and

Eug: When would my docent training begin? It must be nice to be the youngest member of the docent staff . . .

Even while testifying in the U.S. House of Representatives, I knew I could no longer serve in the White House, but I'd hoped my career in the army would continue. I was only forty-four. Even if I had to accept changes in my role, I expected to contribute in a major way to the active military service of the country in the most serious international situations.

With the doors around me abruptly closing, I did my best to get the kind of assignment for which I'd long proven myself suited. I had the credentials, yet suddenly I found it hard to get them documented. Normally, upon leaving the National Security Council, I would have received the Defense Senior Service Medal, an important and distinguishing award. I didn't receive it, presumably because the White House wouldn't sign off on it. Showing one's evaluations is also important to landing the right assignment. On tracks like mine, higher-ups will sign an evaluation endorsing an officer's potential for one day becoming a general officer. Before my testimony, a signature like that would have been easy for me to get. Now no active-duty officer at the highest levels wanted to put a signature on my evaluation.

In the end, I was assigned to the U.S. Army Nuclear and Countering Weapons of Mass Destruction Agency. This served the army's eagerness to get me well out of the way, a motive that was underscored when my orders to transfer to USANCA arrived with non-army-like speed. Still, the new job would allow me to make some real contributions before starting my War College assignment. USANCA works on integrating nuclear weapon effects into joint operations and integrating nuclear deterrence into defense policy. I was to work closely with the technical experts there—good people—on operations and strategy. Also, colonels at USANCA were willing to attach their names to my evaluations.

Yet even as I took the job at USANCA, my head had started to spin a bit. This was late February 2020. For the first time since the crisis began on July 25, 2019, I couldn't see a clear path forward. Navigation is everything, and I didn't know where I was.

What I did know was that I had about ten weeks of vacation stored up. In keeping with the overall army goal of lowering my profile, General Gericke had advised me to take it easy for a bit, so I took six weeks off.

I wasn't planning to take it all that easy. I wanted to get a handle on what I might expect from the rest of my career as an officer. For the first time, I was starting to question whether I really had a viable future, a useful future, in the army. In late January, I'd traveled to a European Foreign Area Officer Symposium hosted by the commander of U.S. Army Europe. There, I had several conversations with senior officers, and although many dozens of my peers, colonel rank and below, were highly supportive of me, the generals I spoke to were pessimistic about my future in the military.

Still, I was only asking myself the question, and tentatively at that. The fact is that I couldn't imagine being out of the army.

On leave, I did spend some time reaching out to people who might have other ideas for me. I contacted heads of think tanks, exploring what my Russia, Ukraine, and military expertise might have to offer. I got good responses, although they were often accompanied by a refrain: *We may need to see what happens with the upcoming presidential election before we formally offer you a position.* I also looked at the academic world and had positive responses from some leading institutions. There were certain consulting companies where I could clearly be of use while making a very good living. But this all felt so strange to me. I knew I should try to understand the various options, just in case I had to retire from the army. In truth, however, I was clinging to the idea that there was a path that would allow me to stay in.

Then came the global pandemic.

As with everyone else in the United States and around the world, the rapid, strange adjustments in daily life that began in the first months of the pandemic will always have a weird, even confused place in my memory. I was by no means the only person confronting dynamic and shifting real-life challenges when they were suddenly thrown into an overarching situation for which they couldn't be fully prepared, a situation requiring quick, thorough changes in normal routines. At the time the pandemic hit, my family was watching as my career prospects outside the military plunged from potentially rosy to totally and completely uncertain.

When I started my leave, in late February, President Trump was downplaying the pandemic and assuring the public that a return to normalcy was just around the corner—despite knowing otherwise. At NSC, we'd been aware as early as January that this virus would be serious, but that it would also be manageable if the president and his administration acted responsibly. Forty days later, when I came back off leave in early April, the country was in complete chaos. The president, once again focused on bolstering his reelection by not spooking the financial markets, had completely mismanaged the crisis. Hundreds, then thousands, then tens of thousands, then hundreds of thousands would die while Trump denied responsibility for the tragedy and even claimed victory over the rampant virus.

For me, the pandemic amplified the sheer strangeness of my new situation. I'd recently been right at the heart of developing U.S. global strategy, and now the nation and the world were in peril. Experts were doing their best, over and against denigration by President Trump, to organize national and local responses; everywhere on the ground, essential workers were making extraordinary sacrifices. The global situation was persistently tense—and yet I wasn't contributing anything at all.

At the same time, I felt I had to stay on top of the immediate challenges to my army career. One of the discussions I had with General Gericke had to do with my promotion to colonel. He even asked me to come in, during my leave, to discuss it. I didn't know it yet, but this promotion question was about to turn into my final wrangle with President Trump and his minions.

By the end of the meeting with General Gericke, it was clear that the promotion board had selected me for promotion to full colonel, an important change in status—and in pay. This gave me at least one thing I had hoped I could count on. There was, however, an obvious issue to consider: President Trump's likely interference with my promotion, in revenge for my testimony.

The army was mindful of the president's vindictiveness. After all, he'd already set a precedent of inserting himself into low-level administrative military matters when he considered it beneficial to his personal interests. Political appointees had rapidly rotated out of positions, military officers had been fired, and even certain unit-level military awards had been rescinded by order of the president when he became unhappy with the recipients.

So General Gericke and I thought it through. Even with my selection by the promotion board secured, I might be on the promotion list or not, or maybe not on the list but added later, or maybe not promoted for eighteen months—just to give the army time to see what happened in the 2020 presidential election. As the general and I gamed it out, we realized that if the president balked at my inclusion on it, the whole list might get held up, negatively affecting the lives of other officers.

So was this my cue to retire? The president was after me and me alone, not the other officers on the list. If I took myself out of the equation, I would at least free up others' promotions. But General Gericke assured me that there would be no long-range problem. He seemed confident the army would handle it and fight for me. He was wrong.

It was in May that I hit a wall—May 5, to be exact. Rachel was preparing food for a family Cinco de Mayo party, and she came up to my office and found me sitting in a chair staring into space.

She asked me what was wrong. I admitted that I didn't know what to do next. With my leave over, I was now back to work at USANCA, but thanks to COVID-19, it was all teleworking—so there I was, at home. All through April, I'd been waiting for the promotion list to come out. It still hadn't. Despite having a lot of support, all of it outside the Department of Defense, I wasn't sure how to turn that support into opportunity.

This painful state of unknowing was a new experience for me. Having to consider all the negative possible scenarios for my future had finally started to get to me. People are surprised when I tell them that there was a long period when I didn't know what to do, or how we would provide for our family, but that was very much the reality—as it has been for many of those forced out of work by Trump and his enablers.

By the middle of the month, I knew that the promotions list

really should have come out by then. Was my promotion causing the delay? Then I was informed that the president's front office, called the Staff Secretary, or StaffSec, had asked that the army's colonel promotion list be passed to them as soon as NSC received it.

The promotion question—along with the question of what might happen to the whole list—now became the most immediate and unsettling of the great unknowns I'd brought on myself, on my family, and even on my fellow officers—some of whom were in urgent situations and needed to know whether they'd been promoted. For the first time, I didn't have a strategy. I couldn't calculate the risks involved in any of the actions available to me. Feeling dependent on an outcome that was beyond my control to affect, I felt paralyzed, trapped.

Rachel, as usual, had a clear view. There were few realistic options for me in the army now, and they all looked like major comedowns from what I'd been doing my whole career. While there was undoubtedly high risk in retiring, and especially in leaving without being promoted to colonel, I knew I could find fulfilling employment and explore new avenues in my areas of expertise in the civilian world.

Pull the plug now: that was Rachel's position. The army has abandoned you. If it's inevitable, don't wait. Rachel's a sharp strategist. And as many spouses would have, she also felt the army's betrayal acutely.

By now, though, I'd spent a long time fully committed to letting the promotion issue work its way through the system. I really wanted my name on that list. I was proud of my selection for War College. I wanted to believe the army was fighting for me, and I found it very hard to let go. I'll admit that I spent some days in May in a state that can only be described as sheer self-pity.

Still, the day after Rachel and I had our Cinco de Mayo conversation, I started getting serious about activating my networks. For one thing, I thought hard about a conversation I'd had at the European Foreign Area Officer Symposium in late January, with Lt. Gen. Charles W. Hooper, the highest-ranking FAO and director of the Defense Security Cooperation Agency, who had sent me a personal letter of support for my testimony. "Don't push on closed doors," General Hooper advised me. It was just a plain fact, he made clear, that I would never again be able to serve as an FAO for Eurasia. I could work in other places, but they wouldn't be strategically important. True, a change in presidential administration in 2021 would remove direct retaliation, but the domestic politics I'd been drawn into would undermine my ability to operate effectively with counterparts in other countries. If I did get my promotion, I might put together a pretty cushy career as a colonel, but I'd never do anything important again. I also pondered my conversation with Gen. Christopher Cavoli, who told me that I, like Icarus, had flown too close to the sun, had likely pissed off senior military leaders, and would need to prove myself in a rehabilitative assignment before I could be trusted to serve again in positions of critical importance. This didn't bode well for continued service.

And in May, we couldn't know that President Trump would be defeated for reelection. Should he prevail in the 2020 election, we knew, my career would be further subject to his wrath and that of his sycophants in politics and the media. I knew I would never be able to be compliant or moderate in response to that kind of ongoing retaliation.

I'd been looking everywhere for lifelines, grasping at reasons to think I could stay in the army and have an exciting and useful future. But I was beginning to see that those lifelines were illusory.

Some retired higher-ups I spoke with told me I should stay. Retired general David Petraeus was one: he advised me not to retire, but he seemed to be taking an older approach, possibly outworn, in which everything would be okay in the end. With Trump still in office, it wouldn't be okay in the end. In any event, the idea of marking time in a do-nothing sinecure, waiting until normal retirement age, was just too depressing for me to accept.

Then, on June 8, I received my prenotification of the order to move to War College. Only a few months earlier, that message would have amplified the thrill of a lifetime. Now it only underscored my growing dilemma. To commit to War College is to commit to the army for three more years, and I still had no idea of my promotion status, no idea of whether I would end up literally manning that radar station in Alaska—one senior military officer had suggested that, in a second Trump administration, I would—no idea whether such exile might even look good compared to likely persecution and potential prosecution in a second Trump term. Any way I looked at it now, my long army future looked grim. Waiting three years to face up to the fact that I had to pull the plug—that wasn't a real plan.

But I wanted my promotion—expected it, knew I deserved it. Would the army do the right thing and fight for me? Would the army be fair to all the other officers involved by releasing the promotion list even with my name on it? I wanted to know. I put myself and my family through a long, hard month of waiting to find out about the list.

Meanwhile, as we now know from reporting in the press that

started later that June, the White House was engaging in yet another low game of political chicanery, at the expense of the military processes of this country, in order to prevent my promotion. The army had forwarded to Mike Esper, the secretary of defense, the list of officers who had been board-approved for promotion. My name was on it. Secretary Esper then floated it to the White House, but the White House had already told the Pentagon officials who handle the list that the president wanted me denied promotion. This gave Esper and the Defense Department a problem. Months before, the White House had developed a six-point memorandum accusing me of wrongdoing; the Defense Department had quietly conducted an investigation into these accusations and found the White House claims completely unsubstantiated.

Now Mark Meadows, the president's chief of staff, was calling in the secretaries of the army and of defense and berating them for not fabricating dirt that would exclude me from the promotions list. People at NSC had been telling the Defense Department that they had evidence of misconduct on my part: Joe Wang, having begun the whisper campaign against me back in the summer of 2019, had doubled down on these claims in the winter to secure a more senior position in the Trump White House. Only months later, he would be whisked out of the White House himself, possibly for failing to deliver evidence sufficient to block my promotion.

While Trump's and Meadows's plan to smear me failed, there was still no action on moving the promotions list forward. The army and the Defense Department weren't doing anything to make it happen. I only later found out about the spurious investigation: they'd conducted it without my knowledge, and it had exonerated me, and yet they had failed to push back against those false White House accusations. Mike Esper would later give an interview to

Politico, defending me and saying he'd backed me. He'd been prepared to resign over the issue, he claimed. This was an easy claim to make by the time he made it. Still, there were a million ways that he and others could have supported me at the time if they'd really wanted to or had had the guts, but nobody in a position to make a difference did anything of the kind. In that sense, Trump's bullying and intimidation once again worked for him. As in foreign affairs, so in political and everyday life: inaction in the face of corruption has an inevitable effect.

And in this case, the effect wasn't just on me. Hundreds of military officers were living in suspense about their promotions.

At last, I knew I had to act.

I did what I'd always done. I fell back on my training. In the first week of July, I carried out what the military calls a "mission analysis," gaining an understanding of both the friendly and the enemy situations, assessing the terrain, imagining the various possible end states. Without mission analysis, no effective planning is possible. I already had some clear intelligence. Now I had to coordinate my observations into an action plan.

My observations: The army as an institution is fundamentally and naturally conservative. The senior generals were unhappy with my public profile. Every future decision regarding my career would be filtered through the impeachment narrative. Even if I were eventually promoted, I would get only easy assignments. Making a three-year commitment to War College, at this point, was a risk even with a Biden victory. With a Trump victory, it would be a manifest disaster.

Counter to those observations were my hopes and worries. Dejected at the prospect of leaving the army after twenty-one years, and sensitive to the risks of doing so, I'd fallen into decision paralysis. But I knew better than that. I'd learned a lot of lessons. One of them was don't self-deter.

My choice was becoming clear. I could continue hanging on to something that was, in stark fact, over—or I could take command of my own destiny. I could assume the army was the only place where I might thrive—or I could retain confidence in my skill set. I could procrastinate in the face of the great unknown—or I could have faith in my gut, knowing I'd find some way to put my skills to use. I could wander in confusion down a familiar but increasingly dark path—or I could start over.

Start over and keep starting over—I'd learned that lesson long before I joined the army. I learned it from my dad. And starting over would be far easier for me than it had been for him. I wasn't a widower with three kids, arriving in a country where I didn't speak the language and with no job prospects. And I had a lot more than $759: I had an Ivy League education, a stellar twenty-one-year military career, high-level experience in foreign policy, the respect of great mentors, and the love and support of millions of my fellow citizens for doing my duty.

I was incredibly lucky. I was a child of the great American Dream. That's what my father gave me.

And the dream was still alive within me. Neither I nor any other citizen of this country is ever supposed to be some puppet jerking on a string at the whim of a terminally irresponsible leader. Holding up the promotions list—that was nothing but bullying. And as I learned in Brooklyn long ago, there's only one way to deal with a bully. The army and the Defense Department leadership might have been intimidated. I wasn't.

My adrenaline was pumping. I'd assessed my situation and myself. The unknown challenges beckoned. I declared myself ready to fight.

On July 8, 2020, I submitted my retirement paperwork.

Two days later, as might have been predicted, the promotions list was positioned for public release. Now that it didn't matter, my name was on it. Nice timing: as soon as they knew I was gone, everybody jumped at the chance to appear as if they'd done the right thing.

I went on Twitter and posted a notice that I'd retired. (It no doubt annoyed senior military leadership when my tweet got 250,000 likes.) I'd submitted my request for retirement on a Wednesday morning; on Friday afternoon, I received my DD 214, the official document certifying my release from active duty. I sat in a chair in my living room and read a one-page summary of the past twenty-one years, six months, and ten days of my life.

It was surreal how fast the paperwork was coming. Processing out of the army usually takes six months at best, but I had my DD 214 in two days and my preliminary out-processing the Monday after I submitted my paperwork.

On Thursday, Major General Gericke called me. He was in Bangkok traveling with General McConville, and while he was calling under the pretext of checking in, his real reason was no secret to me: he wasn't happy that I'd suggested in the press that my next assignment might be manning a radar station in Alaska.

I told him that such a suggestion had been made to me.

He replied, "But we were taking care of you, Alex."

That's when I told him that, as I had been informed just two days before, Secretaries McCarthy and Esper had been called into Mark Meadows's office and told to dig up dirt on me in order for the

White House to justify denying my promotion. I asked him if this was true. He told me that there had indeed been an investigation—this was the first time anyone had made me aware of it—but that I'd been cleared. And he reiterated that the army had been taking care of me. I pushed back and told him that at no point had any serving senior leader reached out providing any encouragement.

At that moment I knew I'd made the right decision. The army and the entire Defense Department, it appeared, were not above conducting sham investigations in order to please this commander in chief.

Less than three weeks later, with speed unprecedented in the army—army personnel would tell me they'd never seen anything like it—I had my final out-processing paperwork in my hands and my military retiree ID card in my wallet. The speed came from above: with me out of the way, the army wouldn't be a target of White House pressure to retaliate. General Gericke's boss, Gen. Charles Flynn, had personally signed my retirement award, a Legion of Merit, on the Monday after the Friday I received my retirement orders—just two days after I submitted my retirement request—and then had assigned a dedicated administrative assistant to walk my papers through and get the job done. And just like that, my career as an army officer was over.

The fast pace of my exit was okay with me. I had a new plan.

August 1, 2020, was my first day as a civilian, and that day I published an op-ed in the *Washington Post*. In the essay, I called out the president for tyranny and for his egregious mishandling of the COVID-19 threat and I announced my intention to serve the country in a whole new context. I would bring my professional and military expertise, and my commitment to telling the truth, to openly resisting both the president's attacks on the Constitution and the national climate of deadly hate and bigotry on which those attacks had fed.

The piece drew over one million reads. This was the beginning of something.

The life I'm living today still involves an enormous amount of uncertainty. It's all new to me. Yet I have confidence that Rachel, Ellie, and I will be okay. I've found employment opportunities of various kinds, and I'm pursuing them eagerly. After twenty-one years in a single, powerfully organized institution, I'm essentially a freelancer now, piecing together jobs: consultant, Eurasia expert, writer, speaker. At the same time, I'm pursuing advanced academic studies in policy at Johns Hopkins University—the only thing I had lined up when I pulled the trigger and retired. I can now discern a future in which I might be back in a senior government position in foreign relations officialdom. And I have some hope of one day again applying my immersion in the history and current politics of Russia and eastern Europe, and in great power competition, to promote greater security and stability for the United States.

But not now. My immediate goal is to address the threats to this country, at home and abroad, that arise from undermining our best national purposes. I didn't get my army promotion. I've given myself a promotion: I serve the country in a new way now.

I never had any intention of becoming a public figure. When I reported the president's wrongdoing, I had no expectation that the wrongdoing itself would become public. Then it did, and very quickly I had to overcome my anxiety and get comfortable making public statements I never would even have considered making before. It was President Trump, not I, who made me and my career a political issue.

I'm not fearful, and I won't be silent. As an immigrant to the United States, a beneficiary of the American Dream, and one who has served the country his whole career, I will continue to clarify, for the public who came so heartwarmingly to my support during my testimony, the crucial importance to the United States of the professionalism and expertise we have at our disposal as a great nation—the commitment to public service, both military and civilian, that President Trump derided and degraded and tried to hollow out at every turn. We have the ability to do amazing things to relieve unfairness and misery, here and around the world. That ability is under vicious attack by forces of hate, ignorance, greed, and criminality.

During my military career, I was given a unique chance to see, up close, the best and the worst of what this country can be. I've paid a price for that knowledge, but my family and my career taught me powerful lessons in commitment, in courage, in real leadership, and in having a true moral compass. We all have those capabilities. That's why I'm an advocate for public service, for a revival of genuine patriotism, for ethical leadership, and for standing up to bullies.

I know we can do it. Whatever I'm working on at any given moment, my aim now is the renewal of this country. Because here, right matters.

EPILOGUE

On the one-year anniversary of President Trump's call with President Zelensky, I reflected on my place in the events that led to his first impeachment. Thanks to a congressional investigation, Trump was unable to carry out his plan to force Ukraine to smear now-president Biden. I believe my role in preventing that attempt, as well as in exposing it to the public, played a part in Trump's defeat in the 2020 presidential election. As I considered the loss of my army and foreign policy career, and the challenges that my family faced thanks to the Trump administration's reprisals, I came to some conclusions that have brought me a degree of acceptance.

In the period immediately after the call, I believed good counsel from senior advisors would be enough to get President Trump to reverse course. It bothered me for a while to wonder what I might have done if Zelensky really *had* decided to conduct an investigation into the Bidens in exchange for a White House visit and the release of U.S. security assistance. But that's a counterfactual that I don't have to live with. Zelensky never conducted such an investigation, in part because congressional inquiries forced the president to lift his hold on the security assistance and because a whistleblower complaint exposed the president's schemes.

I've come to realize that the system worked largely as it was supposed to. Good actors did their duty, obeyed their oaths, and defended the Constitution.

Still, a campaign of bullying, intimidation, and retaliation ended my military career. Following my complaint, the Department of Defense conducted an investigation into my performance as an officer, based on a White House six-point memorandum indicating that I shouldn't be promoted. Simultaneously, White House cronies searched for a way to give me a poor performance review and permanently tank my career.

Despite the unfairness of how my military career ended, I'm at peace with the new phase of my life. Though I am deeply disappointed in the military's tacit complicity in the presidential retaliation, I still love and respect the U.S. Army and the Department of Defense as great American institutions. And while I have left government service, I still consider myself a public servant. My goals now are to help hold accountable those leaders who fail to live up to their oaths, to promote ethical leadership and public service, and to advocate for the national security policies that I believe advance the interests of the United States.

In pursuing those goals, I'm drawing on lessons I've learned, both from challenging experiences and from the great colleagues and leaders I've been privileged to work with. I think many of these lessons can serve as guidelines in personal and professional life. Some also have resonance for the strategies and tactics of great nations like ours. Here they are.

Start Over—and Keep Starting Over

I didn't want to start over. I loved what I did. But I found I couldn't allow my love of military life and my dedication to serving the country's foreign relations stand in the way of reporting the president's improper actions and testifying to them. And so I risked my career. As hard as it was to come to terms with leaving the army, I must have known, deep down, that I was capable of starting over—and of starting over again, should duty or opportunity require it. The legacy of my ancestors' response to the Nazi invasion of Ukraine, my father's courage in fleeing the Soviet Union and bringing us to the United States, the moment when I had to pick myself up after my failure at college and recommit to higher learning, my leaving a successful combat track to become a foreign area officer: those inheritances and experiences held me in good stead when I faced the daunting prospect of starting over. More often than we fully realize, the United States, too, has had to start over. Our unity has at times been very seriously threatened, both from without and from within; our democracy has verged on failure. If we recognize that it's been part and parcel of our history as Americans to start over—to build back better—we can do it again.

Commit to Your Passion(s)

For me, personal discipline was born in discovering the passion that begins in excitement, develops in response to intense demands, inspires creative solutions, results in satisfaction, and leads to further challenges. First came training soldiers in Korea. Then came the test of combat in Iraq. And then the highest challenge: coordinating national policy and deploying my expertise in great nations' conflicts. Facing the sudden end of my military career, I committed just as fully to a new passion: defeating Donald Trump and electing Joe Biden. Being a public figure didn't sit comfortably with me. Yet reaching as many Americans as I could, through many media engagements, became my driving purpose. I discovered a new discipline in that passion. Offered the opportunity to speak at the Democratic National Convention, I demurred. It didn't seem right—retiring from the military and then, only weeks later, speaking in scripted form at a partisan event. My real passion has always been to find my own way.

Navigation Is Everything

I was a natural at navigation in military training and combat: when I heard the president make his proposal that day, I saw my path. Navigation became far more difficult when I found myself unexpectedly operating in the bewildering landscape of congressional testimony. I did eventually find a path through hostile questioning by Republican members of the House, and through the barrage of scurrilous media coverage of my service and background. But when navigating issues surrounding my army promotion, I was too deep in the weeds for too long; I couldn't get map-and-compass bearings. Rachel was the better navigator. She saw early on that there was no realistic way past the obstacles I faced; her advice was to save time, energy, and pain by changing course early. I put my family through a long period of struggle due to my inability to see what Rachel could. Many of us will be blinkered that way at some point—especially when facing the loss of something we're passionately committed to. In the end, I activated networks and made changes. Navigation is everything; imperfect navigation, though a cause of trouble, doesn't have to be often fatal.

There Are People Here

I've said I wasn't born knowing how to do the right thing in a crisis: I had to learn my moral compass, and I think that's done only in relation to other people. Some of the people I've learned from are the soldiers I led in training and in combat and my fellow officers, some of whom gave the last measure of devotion and died in combat. I learned as well from my fellow professionals, both military and civilian: the superb officers and policy experts who encouraged me to find my voice and speak my mind. Most important, of course, has been my family. As we began our American journey, I relied on my twin brother and our older brother, our dad, our grandmother, and our mom; they still sustain me. Rachel is the person crucial to my life, keeping me grounded, making me laugh, supporting and questioning my decisions and helping me think things through. Our struggles with Rachel's pregnancies, and the joy and then the crushing loss of our baby, Sarah, tightened our marital bond. So has parenting our beloved Ellie, as we take joy in her growing and becoming her own person. The moral compass that I hope to pass on to Ellie was formed in these close relationships.

Know Your Role

I've had responsibilities above my official rank, and at first, I wasn't perfectly comfortable and had to will myself to take on what I knew I could do. I learned to be confident in my role from superiors who encouraged me to take chances and seize the initiative. Not that your role will always be the one you've planned for, or most want. When I heard the president make an illicit offer to the head of a foreign government, I wasn't out to become the person who reported it up the line, testified in the third impeachment in U.S. history, aided in preventing a smear against the Biden campaign, became a public figure, and had to begin a whole new career. But that, it turned out, was my role. The United States, too, has had a role of unique strength and responsibility to lead. Because the country often has mixed feelings about that role, Trump was able to do a lot of damage by compromising the integrity of U.S. global leadership, and it's our job now to repair the damage, assess the new possibilities for U.S. leadership, and address the global crises we all face.

Don't Self-Deter

This may be the big one. Nations can self-deter, as I've come to understand from studying U.S.-Russia relations, with unfortunate results. Russia, in an effort to hang on to great power status, assumes the role of a foil to the U.S. and takes aggressive actions that raise the stakes and create a destabilizing sense of high risk. The U.S., keenly aware of the risk—predictably, to the Russians—too often looks only at negative outcomes from action in response to Russian outrages. Thus the U.S. scares itself off, unwittingly accomplishing the Russian purpose. For the greater security of the world, our country shouldn't do that—and individuals shouldn't, either. Overcoming your own discouragement can be a struggle. I didn't falter in the face of risk to my career in reporting presidential misdeeds. But I did, for a time, when I looked into the great unknown that would follow from deciding to retire from the army. In the end, as it was in the army, so it was after the army: I turned out to be my own best advocate. And you are yours.

Where right matters, anyone can do it, and that can change history. Lately I've been thinking a lot about Joshua Chamberlain, a U.S.

army officer in the Civil War. A native of Maine, Chamberlain was teaching rhetoric and languages at Bowdoin College when the Civil War broke out. Unlike many of his peers, he enlisted to fight the secessionist Confederacy. He joined the Army of the Potomac, 20th Maine Regiment, as a lieutenant colonel and was soon promoted to colonel. Through a number of engagements, Chamberlain showed himself a competent officer. Nobody would have thought he'd go down in history.

Then, on July 2, 1863, the second day of the Battle of Gettysburg, with the Union Army scrambling to recover from the previous day's setbacks, Chamberlain was assigned the task of holding a small hill, called Little Round Top, against an opportunistic assault from below. The danger to the United States was deadly serious. Robert E. Lee's Army of Northern Virginia had crossed the Potomac and easily advanced to Gettysburg. If the Confederates weren't stopped here, the advance would continue, possibly all the way to Philadelphia, giving Lee an enormous advantage in negotiating an end to the war on terms favorable to the Southern secession.

Nothing in history is foreordained. Confederate victory was possible. If the 20th Maine couldn't hold the position, the Confederacy would enjoy victory at Gettysburg and have a clear path northward. The Union soldiers trying to hold the hill were battered, driven back on themselves, taking casualties, and running out of ammunition.

In that desperate situation, Chamberlain made a creative and unorthodox decision. He ordered his left wing to undertake a bayonet charge—running downhill into the fire of the advancing enemy, using an unusual wheeling motion, at once flanking and assaulting. This was a risky move. There was no guarantee of success. But going on trying to hold the line by firing diminishing ammunition might have spelled defeat for the United States.

Chamberlain's risk paid off. The 20th Maine's bayonet charge drove the Confederate troops back from Little Round Top. The Union line held. Lee would make another attempt to advance the next day, with further dramatic results, but on July 4 he retreated across the Potomac; he would never again invade the North. Chamberlain's decision for a bayonet charge has justly been credited with turning the tide of the Civil War in the east.

Tide-turning drama like that won't occur in most people's lives, of course. But that's not why we read history. The point of Chamberlain's story is that this wasn't somebody destined for greatness. Nor was he eager for fame in the annals of history as a great American. Placed in an intensely challenging situation, with very high stakes, he was able to rise to the occasion. He drew on training, instincts, and creativity. His decision not to self-deter, to trust himself, saved America.

As we move together out of the national disaster that was the Trump presidency, I'm inspired by the story of Joshua Chamberlain. I think we all, in our own way, have it in us to be like him.

ACKNOWLEDGMENTS

There are many people who helped to make this book possible but none more so than my agent, Christy Fletcher. She understood my vision from the beginning, and this project would never have been possible without her understanding, kindness, and expertise. Likewise, thanks to Jonathan Jao for patiently guiding me through the process. I hope we can meet in person soon! Thanks also to the team at Harper.

Although the concept of the book was easy to develop on my own, Bill Hogeland spent hours listening to my story and helping me to outline and develop the narrative. Thank you, Bill, for making this book what it is.

The military made me who I am. I couldn't possibly name every person who made a lasting impact on me so I won't attempt it. I know some supported and defended me in large and small forums, and it meant everything to me. I especially want to acknowledge three of my best army friends: Carlos, my favorite mentee; Bob, the best travel and Call of Duty partner a guy could ask for; and Victor, who is quite simply my oldest and dearest friend.

Thank you to all my NSC, State, and department and agency colleagues who struggled during a difficult administration but remained steadfast in the oath they took to protect and defend the Constitution of the United States of America and especially to those who paid tremendous consequences for doing the right thing.

Even though I knew I had truth and right on my side, I had an exceptional legal team to help me navigate each phase of the process. Their concern and care for my family and me was as meaningful as their legal help. Thank you to Steve for your loyalty, tough love, and willingness to take me down—literally—when needed; to Matt for your calm demeanor and photo bombing skills; to Michael—The Wolf—for your tenacity, friendship, humor, and generosity; and to David for your wise counsel and always having my best interests in mind.

I am grateful to my friend Rabbi Bruce Aft, who reminded me to ask myself the questions of Rabbi Hillel, "If I am not for myself, who will be for me? And being only for myself, what am 'I'? And if not now, when?" Thank you for your humor and the genuine care you have shown to our family. We have been tremendously blessed by the outpouring of support from our synagogue family at Adat Reyim.

Eug and Cindy . . . it's hard to know what to say. Because of the Great Kitchen Disaster, we were living in your basement when most of the backstory was developing, and that sums up who you are for us: always willing to step in and help in any way. Yes, we all get on each other's nerves from time to time, but people who love one another often do. The best decision I ever made was letting you split off from me, Eug, and your best decision was marrying

Cindy. As your older brother, I always wanted to see you settled and happy, and Cindy has given you that.

Thank you to my older brothers, Len and Alex, for your impact on my formative years and throughout my life.

There are many family members and people who are like family who have encouraged us time and time again: the Bekkers, the Epelbaums, the Kitmans, the Greenmount Gang, and the Saturday Night Zoom Crew. My faithful Oklahoma Fan Club members the Grahams and the Colliers, Susie, Hope, and Ma, who at ninety-four lets us know anytime she hears someone say something nice about me.

Being forced to leave a good and steady job in the middle of a global pandemic and economic downturn was a tough decision but, it was made possible by the kindness of so many who took time to offer their counsel and support. I would especially like to thank Kurt Campbell and his generous friends, Benjamin Wittes, Eliot Cohen, Jennifer Pritzker, Dave Pellizon, and the teams at the Pritzker Military Foundation, Lawfare, the Perry World House, and the Renew Democracy Initiative.

As I have said before, I had the confidence I would be fine because of the example my father gave us. Dad, thank you for being brave, thank you for your perseverance, thank you for your belief in us, thank you for your love, and thank you for giving us a "new mom." Mom, thank you for being an excellent example of devotion and service.

My favorite name outside of "Daddy" is "Uncle." Thank you to Max, Madison, JohnDavid, Madi, Audrey, Ben, Cora, Rowan, Sadie, Ari, and Elias for giving me this title, and to your parents, Eugene, Cindy, JJ, Michelle, Pat, Peyton, Dave, Laura, Brian, and Jane.

Thank you to everyone who sent emails, messages on social media, cards, letters, gifts, and donations in my name. I never regretted the decisions I made, but there were some lonely and uncertain days. I am humbled by your thoughtfulness. Your kindness buoyed our family.

Finally, I would like to thank all who paid the ultimate price in service to our nation. Their sacrifice will always be my greatest inspiration. May their memories be a blessing.

ABOUT THE AUTHOR

LIEUTENANT COLONEL ALEXANDER S. VINDMAN (RET.) was most recently the director for European Affairs on the White House's National Security Council. Prior to retiring from the U.S. Army, he served as a foreign area officer with assignments in U.S. embassies in Kyiv, Ukraine, and Moscow, Russia, and for the chairman of the Joint Chiefs of Staff as a Political-Military Affairs officer. He is currently a doctoral student and a Foreign Policy Institute fellow at the Johns Hopkins School of Advanced International Studies, a Pritzker Military fellow at the Lawfare Institute, a board member of the Renew Democracy Initiative nonprofit, and a visiting fellow at the University of Pennsylvania's Perry World House.